SHIA
CRESENT

EMERGENCE OF
WORLD WAR 3

JAMAI HAQUANI

Outskirts Press, Inc.
Denver, Colorado

Shia Cresent
Emergence of World War 3

Outskirts Press, Inc.
http://www.outskirtspress.com

ISBN: 978-1-4327-1858-9

Outskirts Press and the "OP" logo are trademarks belonging to Outskirts Press, Inc.

PRINTED IN THE UNITED STATES OF AMERICA

Nuclear Capable Iran could give rise to a Shia dominance in the Middle East spanning from Iran to the Mediterranean and eventually threaten the European region and the west, and thereby causing the entire region to be monopolized by fanatics like President Mahmood Ahmedinejad and Mullahs who subscribe to a Fundamentalist Arm of the Shia sect that envisions the end of the World. If we allow Iran to become Nuclear Capable, we may see the dawn of a heinous era leading United States and the allies and other nations involved into World War Three.

I dedicate this book to my Spiritual Teachers, for all the
Wisdom they shared with me.
I am forever grateful

Contents

Preface

In writing this book I aim to shed new light on the Iranian Nuclear standoff with the west. My research prior to writing this book truly gave me the sense that Iran would be key in shaping the next century, and that the Shia hegemony in the region was a real possibility. After the first gulf war I began researching the middle east and southern Asia. Soon after Pakistan disclosed its nuclear program and detonated a nuclear bomb in the northern mountains of Pakistan and the world witnessed a new member into the nuclear club, I predicted that Iran would be next and somehow Pakistan would aid Iran in achieving a nuclear bomb. Even though Pakistan is contained at the moment by a military dictator, it is a bullet away from disaster. As I wrote this book I realized that the fundamentalist in Pakistan are hard at work plotting to overthrow or assassinate Gen. Musharraf, so they can get their hands on the nuclear trigger. I feel it is just a matter of time. Unlike its neighbor Iran would not be contained or reasoned with that easily. Iranian regime has one goal since late Ayatollah Khomeni overthrew the shah in 1979, that is to build a Shia empire spanning from Iran to the Mediterranean and wipeout its arch enemy Israel and eventually aim its weapons to Europe and the United States. The ultimate goal of Khomeni was to destroy the super power status of the United States. According to the Khomeni doctrine Britain and United States are the new faces of the Crusaders that returned and broke up the Ottoman Empire and are now wanting to rule the Middle East and its resources. One thing is for certain if the world community allows Iran to acquire nuclear weapons, I am certain it would unlock the gates to World War Three. This may be the time to stop Iran and the chaos that could follow.

Chapter 1

A brief history of the Shiite movement

The term Shia literally means to split from, or cause, a sect. The second largest sect in Islam takes its very name from this word. By most estimates Sunnis make up approximately about 85 percent of the worlds Muslim population, with shias accounting for the rest. When individuals speak of sectarianism in Islam, these two names, which are rooted in the earliest days of the Islamic Caliphate, are the most often mentioned. For sake of comparison it is similar to the great Protestant-Catholic divide in Christianity. The division didnt happen until well over a thousand years in Church, the great Shia Sunni division came within the lifetime of the surviving companions of the Prophet Muhammad and was not focused on doctrinal disputes. The main cause for the existence of the shia sect points to the election of Abu Bakr the first Caliph of the Muslim community in the year 632. After the passing of Prophet Muhammad the leaders of the

1

Muslim community gathered to appoint a political successor to keep the fledgling Muslim nation united. This had to be done because the Prophet had communicated this on numerous occasions to the Muslims. After and intense debate, Abu Bakr was chosen to be the leader. Ali, the cousin and son-in-law of Prophet Muhammad was not present at the gathering and according to some historians protested the outcome. Once again by some historians he refuse to swear allegiance to Abu Bakr for a few months, eventually he gave in and both his supporters took the oath. This was by some account the early stages of the shia separation. However; and as each new Caliph was elected, Alis friends stood by in anger, watching other men being given the position while the beloved leader was passed over. In 656 when Ali was finally elected as the fourth Caliph, his group felt vindicated. Alis rule was very limited and short-lived, though; and the Shia (as his followers came to be known), who were still just a political party at that time, felt that a clan known a Banu Umayyah had unfairly snatched away the caliphate through war and deception. This gave birth to a permanent divisions. In general, any Muslim who is outside the Shia sect is called a Sunni: a person who follows the tradition and example of Prophet Muhammad and his companions. By a Sunni belief any righteous Muslim can be elected leader or Caliph, not just a descendant of the Prophet. Sectarianism among Sunnis has always been more on the basis of intellectual dispute rather than on practice.The Shias continued their offensive against any who they considered to be usurpers, though they met with little success. By the end of the eighth century the Shia had started to develop doctrines of their own that were distinct. They first reformulated the basis of Islamic law by refuting the legal opinions expressed by most of the companions of the Prophet. This was done on the grounds that anyone who supported a caliph other than Ali and Son-in-law of the Prophet must be a sinner whose legitimacy is null and void. As a result of this the Shias began to compile their own books of legal opinions or hadiths and Quranic interpretations on what they recognized to be the correct view of Islam. Majority of the legal opinions recorded are different or opposite from the ones assembled by the majority community during and shortly after the passing of the Prophet. Variations in how the five pillars of Islam are practiced have crept in also. One of the examples many Shias combine certain prayers so that they actually pray only three times during the, not five. Another area of difference with the majority Sunni community happens in the area of leadership. Sunnis have taken a more relaxed view toward the selection of a leader or the most qualified adult male, Shia doctrine claims that Ali and his male descendants have a secret, almost prophetic, wisdom that is passed on from father to son. They are sinless and are therefore the only choice to rule over the community of Muslims. The early Shia followed Ali as their leader, from many accounts he disapproved of their excessive emphasis of his role. Generations followed his descendants, whom they called their Imams or (Leaders). The sixth Shia Imam, Jafar as Siddiq, is credited with the formulation of the Shias complete legal code called Jafari School of Thought. After Jafars death in 765 the Shia divided into two separate sects, each following one of his tow sons, Musa and Ismail. The Ismaili sect , as it is called today, stopped the line with the latter and went on to develop its own doctrines further. This group held that the Imams were part of a grand cycle of history. In place of the absent Imam, however, leaders who could speak for an awaited savior would govern.(The Aga Khan is currently considered the worldwide head of one of the two existing

Ismaili branches of Shiaism.) The main group of Shias went on to follow five more descendants of Ali and were united as a group in Bagdad during the time of the Abbasid Caliphate. With the death of the eleventh Imam in 874, who left no heirs, the Shias developed the concept of a Twelfth Hidden Imam, who was taken as a baby into another realm of existence. The Hidden Imam would return as a Messiah to liberate the Shias from the oppression heaped upon them. The Shia gradually developed a new leadership or hierarchy consisting of popelike figure to head their community. This individual would lead the masses through priesthood consisting of men with such titles a Ayatullah, Mullah, and Hojatulislam. The late Ayatullah Khomeni, who lead the Iranian Revolution in 1978, received the highest rank in the eyes of the worldwide Shia community and was considered infallible. The Shia term Ayatullah means sign of God. Sunnis have no priesthood or identifiable religious structure. Competing Shia and Sunni political factions have struggled for power all throughout Islamic history. The most clear difference between Shia and Sunni so you the reader can understand in a nut shell is the Shias believe the Caliphate, which they call Imamate, is non-elective, and that the head of the Muslim community must be a descendant of Prophet Muhammad. The Shia hold that the imam inherit the Prophets spiritual knowledge and the ability to interpret Divine Law in its light.

Below are the Twelve Shia Imams in chronological order.

Ali................... 656-661
Hasan................ 661-669
Husayn.............. 669-680
Zayn al-Abidin..... 680-712
Muhammad
Al-Baqir............ 712-c735
Jafar al-Sidiq....... 735-765
Musa al Kazim..... 765-799
Ali al Rida.......... 799-818
Muhammad
Al-Tariq al Jawad.. 818-835
Ali al- Hadi......... 835-868
Hasan al-Askari.... 868-873
Muhammad al Mahdi (The 12[Th] Imam Vanished. The Shia call him the Awaited One.

Chapter 2

Ayatullah Khomeni and the Revolution of 1979

Rouhollah Mousavi Khomeini was born on 24 September 1902 in the small town of Khomein, some 160 kilometres to the southwest of Qom. He was the child of a family with a long tradition of religious scholarship. His ancestors, descendants of Imam Mousa al-Kazim, the seventh Imam of the Ahl al-Bayt, had migrated towards the end of the eighteenth century from their original home in Neishapour (in Khorasan province of Iran) to the Lucknow region of northern India. There they settled and began devoting themselves to the religious instruction and guidance of the regions predominantly Shii population.

Khomeinis grandfather, Seyed Ahmad, left Lucknow (according to a statement of Khomeinis elder brother, Seyed Morteza Pasandideh, his point of departure was Kashmir, not Lucknow) some time in the middle of the nineteenth century on pilgrimage to the tomb of Hazrat Ali in Najaf. While in Najaf, Seyed Ahmad met Yousef Khan, a prominent citizen of Khomein. Accepting his invitation, he decided to settle in Khomein to assume responsibility for the religious needs of its citizens and also took Yousef Khans daughter in marriage.

Seyed Ahmad, by the time of death, the date of which is unknown, had two children: a daughter by the name of Sahiba, and Seyed Moustafa Hindi, born in 1885, the father of Khomeini. Seyed Moustafa began his religious education in Esfahan and continued his advanced studies in Najaf and Samarra (this corresponded to a pattern of preliminary study in Iran followed by advanced study in the Atabat, the shrine cities of Iraq; Ayatollah Khomeini was in fact the first religious leader of prominence whose formation took place entirely in Iran). After accomplishing his advanced studies he returned to Khomein, and then married with Hajar (mother of Rouhollah Khomeini).

In March 1903, Khomeini when was just 5 months old lost his father. And in 1918, Khomeini lost both his aunt, Sahiba, who had played a great role in his early upbringing, and his mother, Hajar. Responsibility for the family then devolved on his eldest brother, Seyed Mourteza (later to be known as Ayatollah Pasandideh).

Khomeini began his education by memorizing the Qoran at a maktab (traditional religious school). In 1920-21, Seyed Mourteza sent the Rouhollah Khomeini to the city of Arak (or Sultanabad, as it was then known) in order for him to benefit from the more ample educational resources available there.

In 1923, Khomeini arrived in Qom and devoted himself to completing the preliminary stage of madreseh (school or academy) education.

Khomeini did not engage in any political activities during the 1930s. He believed that the leadership of political activities should be in the hands of the foremost religious scholars, and he was therefore obliged to accept the decision of Ayatollah Haeri to remain relatively passive toward the measures taken by **Reza Shah** against the traditions and culture of Islam in Iran. In any event, as a still junior figure in the religious institution in Qom, he would have been in no position to mobilize popular opinion on a national scale.

In 1955, a nationwide campaign against the Bahai sect was launched, for which the Khomeini sought to recruit Ayatollah Boroujerdis (he was the most prominent religious leader in Qom after the death of Ayatollah Haeri) support, but he had little success.

Ayatollah Khomeini therefore concentrated during the years of Ayatollah Boroujerdis leadership in Qom on giving instruction in fiqh (Islamic science) and gathering round him students who later became his associates in the movement that led to the overthrow of the Pahlavi Dynasty, not only Ayatollah Mutahhari and Ayatollah Muntaziri, but younger men such as Hojatolislam Muhammad Javad Bahonar and Hojatolislam Ali Akbar Hashimi-Rafsanjani.

The emphases of the Ayatollah Khomeinis activity began to change with the death of Ayatollah Boroujerdi on March 31, 1961, for he now emerged as one of the successors to Boroujerdis position of leadership. This emergence was signaled by the publication of some of his writings on fiqh, most importantly the basic handbook of religious practice entitled, like others of its genre, Tozih al-Masael. He was soon accepted as Marja-e Taqlid by a large number of Iranian Shiis.

In the autumn of 1962, the government promulgated new laws governing elections to local and provincial councils, which deleted the former requirement that those elected be sworn into office on the Qoran. Seeing in this a plan to permit the infiltration of public life by the Bahais, Imam Khomeini telegraphed both the **Mohammad Reza Shah** and the prime minister of the day, warning them to desist from violating both the law of Islam and the Iranian Constitution of 1907, failing which the ulama (religious scholars) would engage in a sustained campaign of protest.

In January 1963, the Shah announced a six-point program of reform called the White Revolution, an American-inspired package of measures designed to give his regime a liberal and progressive facade. Ayatollah Khomeini summoned a meeting of his colleagues in Qom to press upon them the necessity of opposing the Shahs plans. They sent Ayatollah Kamalvand, to see the Shah and gauge his intentions. Although the Shah showed no inclination to retreat or compromise, it took further pressure by Ayatollah Khomeini on the other senior ulama of Qom to persuade them to decree a boycott of the referendum that the Shah had planned to obtain the appearance of popular approval for his White Revolution. Ayatollah Khomeini issued on January 22, 1963 a strongly worded declaration denouncing the Shah and his plans. Two days later Shah took armored column to Qom, and he delivered a speech harshly attacking the ulama as a class.

Ayatollah Khomeini continued his denunciation of the Shahs programs, issuing a manifesto that also bore the signatures of eight other senior scholars. In it he listed the various ways in which the Shah had violated the constitution, condemned the spread of moral corruption in the country, and accused the Shah of comprehensive submission to America and Israel. He also decreed that the **Norooz** celebrations for the Iranian year 1342 (which fell on March 21, 1963) be cancelled as a sign of protest against government policies.

On the afternoon of Ashoura (June 3, 1963), Imam

Khomeini delivered a speech at the Feyziyeh madreseh in which he drew parallels between the Umayyad caliph Yazid and the Shah and warned the Shah that if he did not change his ways the day would come when the people would offer up thanks for his departure from the country. The immediate effect of the Imams speech was, however, his arrest two days later at 3 oclock in the morning by a group of commandos who hastily transferred him to the Qasr prison in Tehran. As dawn broke on June 3, the news of his arrest spread first through Qom and then to other cities. In Qom, Tehran, Shiraz, Mashhad and Varamin, masses of angry demonstrators were confronted by tanks and paratroopers. It was not until six days later that order was fully restored. This uprising of 15 Khordad 1342 marked a turning point in Iranian history.

After nineteen days in the Qasr prison, Ayatollah Khomeini was moved first to the Eshratabad military base and then to a house in the Davoudiyeh section of Tehran where he was kept under surveillance.

He was released on April 7, 1964, and returned to Qom.

The Shahs regime continued its pro-American policies and in the autumn of 1964, it concluded an agreement with the United States that provided immunity from prosecution for all American personnel in Iran and their dependents. This occasioned the Khomeini to deliver a speech against the Shah. He denounced the agreement as surrender of Iranian independence and sovereignty, made in exchange for a $200 million loan that would be of benefit only to the Shah and his associates, and described as traitors all those in the Majlis who voted in favor of it; the government lacked all legitimacy, he concluded.

Shortly before dawn on November 4, 1964, again commandos surrounded the Ayatollah Khomeini house in Qom, arrested him, and this time took him directly to

Mehrabad airport in Tehran for immediate exile to Turkey on the hope that in exile he would fade from popular memory. As Turkish law forbade Ayatollah Khomeini to wear the cloak and turban of the Muslim scholar, an identity which was integral to his being. However, On September 5, 1965, Ayatollah Khomeini left Turkey for Najaf in Iraq, where he was destined to spend thirteen years.

Once settled in Najaf, Ayatollah Khomeini began teaching fiqh at the Sheikh Mourteza Ansari madreseh. At this madreseh he delivered, between January 21 and February 8, 1970, his lectures on Velayat-e faqeeh, the theory of governance and Islamic Leadership (the text of these lectures was published in Najaf, not long after their delivery, under the title Velayat-e faqeeh ya Hukumat-i Islami). The text of the lectures on Velayat-e faqeeh was smuggled back to Iran by visitors who came to see the Khomeini in Najaf.

The most visible sign of the popularity of Ayatollah Khomeini in the pre-revolutionary years, above all at the heart of the religious institution in Qom, came in June 1975 on the anniversary of the uprising of 15 Khordad. Students at the Feyziyeh madreseh began holding a demonstration within the confines of the building, and a sympathetic crowd assembled outside. Both gatherings continued for three days until they were attacked military forces, with numerous deaths resulting. Ayatollah Khomeini reacted with a message in which he declared the events in Qom and similar disturbances elsewhere to be a sign of hope that freedom and liberation from the bonds of imperialism were at hand. The beginning of the revolution came indeed some two and a half years later.

In January 7, 1978 when an article appeared in the semi-official newspaper Ittilaat attacking him in such terms as a traitor working together with foreign enemies of the country. The next day a furious mass protest took place in Qom; it was suppressed by the security forces with heavy loss of life. This was the first in a series of popular confrontations that, gathering momentum throughout 1978, soon turned into a vast revolutionary movement, demanding the overthrow of the Pahlavi regime and the installation of an Islamic government.

Shah decided to seek the deportation of Ayatollah Khomeini from Iraq, the agreement of the Iraqi government was obtained at a meeting between the Iraqi and Iranian foreign ministers in New York, and on September 24, 1978, the Khomeinis house in Najaf was surrounded by troops. He was informed that his continued residence in Iraq was contingent on his abandoning political activity, a condition he rejected. On October 3, he left Iraq for Kuwait, but was refused entry at the border. After a period of hesitation in which Algeria, Lebanon and Syria were considered as possible destinations, Ayatollah Khomeini embarked for Paris. Once arrived in Paris, the Khomeini took up residence in the suburb of Neauphle-le-Chateau in a house that had been rented for him by Iranian exiles in France. From now on the journalists from across the world now made their way to France, and the image and the words of the Ayatollah Khomeini soon became a daily feature in the worlds media.

On January 3, 1979, **Shapour Bakhtiar** of the National Front (Jabhe-yi Melli) was appointed prime minister to replace General Azhari. And on January 16, Shah left Iran. The Ayatollah Khomeini embarked on a chartered airliner of Air France on the evening of January 31 and arrived in Tehran the following morning. He was welcomed by a very popular joy. On February 5, he introduced Mehdi Bazargan as interim prime minister (yet Bakhtiyar was appointed prime minister of Shah).

On February 10, Ayatollah Khomeini ordered that the curfew should be defied. The next day the Supreme Military Council withdrew its support from Bakhtiyar, and on February 12, 1979, following the sporadic street gunfight all organs of the regime, political, administrative, and military, finally collapsed. The revolution had triumphed.

On March 30 and 31, a nationwide referendum resulted in a massive vote in favor of the establishment of an Islamic Republic. Ayatollah Khomeini proclaimed the next day, April 1, 1979, as the first day of Gods government. He obtained the title of Imam (highest religious rank in Shia). With the establishment of Islamic Republic of Iran he became Supreme Leader (Vali-e Faqeeh).

He settled in Qom but on January 23, 1980, Ayatollah Khomeini was brought from Qom to Tehran to receive heart treatment. After thirty-nine days in hospital, he took up residence in the north Tehran suburb of Darband , and on April 22 he moved into a modest house in Jamaran, another suburb to the north of the capital. A closely guarded compound grew up around the house, and it was there that he spent the rest of his life as absolute ruler of Iran.

Ayatollah Khomeini, on June 3, 1989, after eleven days in hospital for an operation to stop internal bleeding, lapsed into a critical condition and died.

Ayatollah Khomeini in his 10 years of leadership established a theocratic rule over Iran. He did not fulfil his pre-revolution promises to the people of Iran but instead he started to marginalize and crash the opposition groups and those who opposed the clerical rules. He ordered establishment of many institutions to consolidate power and safeguard the cleric leadership. During his early years in power he launched the Cultural Revolution in order to Islamize the whole country. Many people were laid off, and lots of books were revised or burnt according to the new Islamic values. Newly established Islamic Judiciary system sentenced many Iranians to death and long-term imprisonment as they were in opposition to those radical changes.

Chapter 3
Iranian Ethnic groups

The official language of Iran is Persian (Farsi). Persian is a West Iranian language of the Indo-European family of languages and is spoken in those parts of Iran where the Fars people, Persians, dwell, as well as in the Republic of Tajikistan. Tehran, Isfahan, Fars, Khorasan, Kerman and Yazd are some of the provinces inhabited by the Persians.

There are a number of other national and ethnic groups living in various parts of Iran. The historical background and anthropological origin of these groups have been subject of numerous research works, but researchers are not unanimous concerning many of the questions posed. '

The most important of these groups with specific history, culture, customs, and language are the Turks, the Kurds, the Baluchis, the Arabs, the Turkmans and the Lurs. There are also a number of ethnic minorities, but they have not been given much anthropological attention for a number of reasons, their small population and their extensive mixing with other Iranians being only two. The following is a general outline of the most populous ethnic and national groups mentioned.

TURKS

There are two streams of opinion concerning the origin of Iranian Turks. The first maintains that they are the descendants of the Turks who either migrated to Iran in the 7th and 11th centuries or invaded parts of Iran at various times. The second holds that they are original inhabitants of Iran on whom the invaders have imposed their languages throughout centuries of occupation. The Iranian Turks live mainly in the north west of Iran in the Eastern and Western Azarbaijan and Ardebil provinces (capitals Tabriz , Urumiyeh and Ardebil respectively), the Zanjan province up to Qazvin, in and around Hamedan, in Tehran, around Qom and Saveh, Khorasan province, and are scattered throughout many other parts of Iran. Some of the central and southern ethnic groups, the Qashqaie for example, are Turkish speaking . '

The Turkish which is spoken in Iran is associated with the Turkish spoken in the Caucasus, but it has undergone varying developments in various regions. The Turkish dialect spoken in both the Azarbaijan province in Iran and in the Republic of Azarbaijan is Oghoz, which is the mother tongue of the Iranian Turks. The Oghoz have two accent groups: the northern and southern. The northern accent is spoken in the Azarbaijan Republic. The southern accent is prevalent in Iran, where the people have been influenced by Farsi. The differences in dialect, and in the culture and customs in particular, among the Turks in Iran has been largely ignored; the emphasis is generally placed on the Turkish language as a whole rather than other characteristics of the Turks in Iran. Several Turkish dynasties have ruled Iran in the past, including the Ghaznavid, Seljuk, Safavids, Qajars. The Turks are thought to be the largest non-Farsi speaking ethnic group in Iran. Back in 1944, a group of left wing nationalists organized the Azarbaijan Democratic Party and established an autonomous government in the Iranian Azarbaijan. They were provided this opportunity by the presence of the Soviet Red Army, who were then a part of the Allied Forces in Iran. During its one-year in office, the nationalist government made Turkish the official language of the region. Upon the withdrawal of the Red Army from Iran, the Iranian army moved in and crushed the rebellion in December 1946.

KURDS

The exact origin of the Kurds has not been yet been researched, even though they have an ancient history. The Kurds reside mainly in Kurdestan. It is a large territory extending to a major part of the mountainous region of southeast Turkey, northeast Iraq, northwest Iran and parts of Russia, as well as Syria.

Up until 1914, the Kurds and Kurdestan were divided among Iran, Russia and the Ottoman Empire. Under a treaty concluded between the Soviet Union and Turkey in 1921, the Kurdish-inhabited region of the Caucasus was annexed to the Ottoman Empire. Subsequently, a part of Kurdestan was placed under Iraqi and Syrian rule when the Mosul region was annexed to Iraq.

In Iran, the Kurds mainly reside in Kurdestan, Kermanshahan, and south of the Western Azarbaijan province. In 1600, a number of the Kurds were forced to settle in the north of Khorasan province, at Quchan and Bojnourd, by the Safavid King, Shah Abbas; they still reside there today.

The Kurds are of Iranian origin. Their language is a North-West Iranian language of the Indo-European family of languages and have several dialects. The two Goorani (southern Kurdish) and Zaza (western Kurdish) dialects are vastly different from Kormanji (pure Kurdish). The dialects spoken in Sanandaj, Kermanshahan, and Suleimania (Iraq) are variations of Kormanji. The Kurds struggle for autonomy and independence dates back to the 19th century, when they were under the Ottoman Empire. Iranian Kurds also rebelled against the central government in 1880.

In 1946, the Peoples Republic of Kurdestan, led by Qazi Mohammad, was established in Iranian Kurdestan, with Mahabad as its capital. The Iranian army crushed the republic when the Red Army pulled out of Iran in the same year.

There are several Kurdish clans. The significant ones are Mokri in the north of Kurdestan, Bani-Ardalan to their south (with Sanandaj as their center), Jaaf in southern and Kalhor in southernmost Kurdestan at the border with Kermanshahan.

Most Kurds are Sunnis of the Shafei, and some are followers of Yazidi and Ahl-e Haq sects, but Qaderi and Naqshbandi brands of Sufism are also common in some parts of the Iranian Kurdestan, particularly in its southern regions. The Kurdish population is estimated to be around 1.5 million.

BALUCHIS

The Baluchis reside mainly in Baluchestan, which is a dry region in the south-eastern part of the Iranian plateau. It extends from the Kerman desert to the rest of Bam and Beshagard mountains, and to the western borderline of the Sind and Punjab provinces of Pakistan. Baluchestan is divided between Iran and Pakistan. Iran and Pakistan had a dispute concerning the border dividing the two parts of Baluchestan, which was resolved by an agreement in 1959. The Iranian Baluchestan is a part of the Sistan and Baluchestan province. Its important towns are Zahedan, Zabol, Iranshahr, Saravan, Chahbahar, etc.

Historically, the Baluchis moved to Makran from Kerman to flee an expedition of the Seljuk in the 11th century. At the time, the Baluchis were nomads. They have never had a centralized government and have been living under a tribal system.

Baluch is the title of several tribes, a small number of which live in the Republic of Turkmenistan. The Baluchis speak Baluchi, which is a West Iranian language of the Indo-European family of languages that has been influenced by the eastern Iranian dialects. It has two branches of northern (Sorhadi) and southern (Makrani) Baluchis. The Iranian Baluch tribes are divided into a number of clans. The most important are the Bameri, Balideh, Bozorgzadeh, Riggi, Sardaar Zaie, Shahbakhsh, Lashari, Mobaraki, Mir Morad Zaie, Naroyee, Nooshsiravani, Barohooyee, Baram-Zehi, and Shir-Khanzayee tribes. The Iranian Baluchis are mostly of the Hanafi sect of the Sunni faith.

A few tribes in the Sistan area are also regarded as Baluch, but they speak Sistani. The language is an abandoned dialect of Persian. The notable ones of these tribes are: Sarbandi, Shahraki, Sargazi, Zamir-Farsyoon, Mir-Arab and Sanjarani.

LURS

Lur is the title of a group of Iranians living in the mountainous areas of the south-west, mainly in Lurestan province. On the basis of historical evidence, the Lur appear to be of the same ethnic origin as the Kurds.

The Luri language is affixed to the old Iranian language, which suggests the length of time that the Lur have lived in Iran. It is close to Kurdish, but is an independent language in its own right. There are four main Lur groups: the Bala Garideh, Delfan, Selseleh and Tarhan. The Bala Garideh are the genuine Lur who are divided into important tribes such as Dirakvand, Janaki, Amaleh, Sagvand, etc.

TURKMANS

The Turkmans are an ethnic minority who speak the Turkish language with the Eastern Oghoz accent. The same dialect is spoken in the Republic of Turkmenistan. They live in the Turkoman Sahra and in the Gorgan plains. The area is a fertile plain near the Iranian border with the Republic of Turkmenistan. It extends from the Atrak river in the north, to the Caspian Sea in the west, Quchan mountains to the east and the Gorgan river to the south.

Iranian Turkmans have been living in Iran since 550 AD, but they first began forming tribes from 750 AD onwards. They are the descendants of Central Asian Turks, who retained their ethnic identity during the Mongol invasion. They were divided among Iran, Russia and Afghanistan in 1885.

Not all the nine Turkoman tribes live in Iran. The most important Iranian Turkoman tribes are Kuklans and Yamotes. The Kuklans have six branches, and live in the central and eastern Turkoman Sahra. The Yamotes have two large clans, the Atabai and Jaafarbai, and live to the west of Turkoman Sahra. There are also smaller tribes to the east of the region in a few villages.

The Turkoman population is estimated to be around one million, and their biggest towns and cities are Gonbad Kavus, which is the center of Turkoman Sahra, Bandar Turkoman, Aq-Qala, and Gomishan. The largest group of Turkman Muslims follow the Hanafi branch of the Sunni sect, but some Turkmans are followers of the Naqshbandieh sufism.

Turkmans have a history of opposition to central governments. One of their significant rebellions was suppressed by the first Pahlavi king, Reza Shah. That defeat, they believe, struck a deadly blow at their national culture.

ARABS

Some historians maintain that the first Arabian tribes migrated to Khuzistan, a section in south-west of Iran where they now live, in the early centuries AD, probably moving in from the Arabian peninsula. Arabian tribes are scattered in an areas between the Arvandroud(Shatt al-Arab) and the Persian Gulf in the south and Shush in the north. Their territory is located to the west of the Bakhtiyari territory , and some of them even mingle with the Bakhtiyari tribe. The most important of the Arabian tribes in Iran is the Bani-Kaab, which is also the largest. Its numerous clans inhabit the Minoo Island, Khorramshahr, Shadegan on both sides of the Karun river, up to around Ahwaz to the north. The House of Kassir people are inhabitants of the city of Ahwaz, west and south of Dezful river and between the Dezful and Shushtar rivers. Other are: Bani-Lam, Bani-Saleh, Bani-Torof, Bani-Tamim, Bani-Marvan, Al-Khamiss, Bavi and Kenane.

The Arabians have retained their Arabic language and many of their old customs, but they have lost some of their ethnological characteristics. Information on the size of Arabian population in Iran is not available. One reason for this is the extensive migration of the people from Khuzistan to other parts of Iran following the Iraqi invasion in 1980. The population census taken in 1976 put the size of the Arabian tribal population at around 300,000.

NOMADS

The migrating nomads constitute a community with a way of living distinct from the urban and rural communities. Two major, related factors prompt them to migrate to winter and summer territories, depending on seasonal changes. The first is their livelihood, and the second is the geographical and climatic conditions they live in.

Historically, however, social and political factors have also been influential in creating this pattern of living. These have included political instability, conflicts between local rulers, heavy tax collection campaigns of urban rulers at times of financial problems, etc. The migratory nomads earn their living principally from raising livestock, although farming and handicraft compliment their main occupation. All other economic activities are insignificant.

This compels them to look for fresh grazing lands. Also, the very cold winters in some regions of Iran and extremely hot summers in others force them to move from winter to summer territories and vice versa to avoid the extreme weather conditions.

CHARACTERISTICS

Over the centuries their communal characteristics have come to take a shape rather different from those of the urban and rural communities. According to the definition the migrating nomads are: a) dependent on livestock raising; b) organized in tribal structure with clear patterns of kinship and relationships; and c) conscious of their tribalism. Furthermore, each tribe has an established territory, with commonly owned grazing lands and with a tribal administrative and social organization.

The nomadic tribes are of several major ethnic origins: Turks, Turkmans, Persians, Kurds, Lurs, Arabs and Baluchis. Hence, they speak a variety of languages and are spread all over the country. Kurdestan and Yazd are the only two provinces without nomadic tribes. But some tribes cross through the latter to get to their winter and summer territories. The Kurdish tribes are in the Bakhtaran province.

CENSUS

The second stage of the latest census taken among the migrating nomads, completed in 1987, showed new results. The total population of nomadic tribes is 1,152,099. There are 597,774 men and 554,325 women. The total number of households is 180,223. The number in the smallest nomadic division, which shall be called the permanent group here for the sake of definition, is 23,606. A permanent group consists of a number of households related either by kinship or by marriage.

The total number of tribes is 96, but there are an additional 547 independent clans. Some of these do have neither a solid tribal structure nor a large number of households. Many of these clans are the remnants of old tribes and clans, which have disintegrated over time or settled in a particular region.

The first stage of the census taken in 1985 had shown that the Kerman and Hormozgan provinces have the highest number of tribes: 28. The largest number of clans, 295 in all, have their territories in the Sistan & Baluchestan and in a part of Khorasan provinces. The highest number of migrating households are in the Chaharmahal & Bakhtiyari, Khuzistan and Isfahan provinces.

CHANGING PATTERNS

The changing economic, political and social structures in the 20th century have caused certain developments in the related tribal patterns. Two factors influenced the changes in the economic field. These were transactions with sedentary urban and rural communities, and the agrarian reforms of the 1960s and 1970s. The reforms undermined the previous organization of production units. As the result, grazing lands were specified to families.

The application of more advanced agricultural tools and the changing organization of farming reduced the importance of the inter-clan family relations.

The disarming of the nomadic tribes, the increased power of the central government and its intervention in tribal affairs, the promotion of labor markets in the regional towns, the rising rate of literacy, the recruitment by government departments, and the expanding urbanization were all factors that contributed to the changes in the social structure of nomadic population.

Migration was also modernized by expansion of roads and the introduction of cars and motorcycles.

SETTLEMENT

Forced settlement of nomadic tribes became a concern of the government under the first Pahlavi king in the 1920s and 1930s. Considering that they had been a source of opposition to central governments in preceding eras, it would have been easier to control them if they settled. Attempts to achieve this were unsuccessful, mainly because they were not accompanied with corresponding measures to provide for the livelihood of nomads.

More attention has been paid to nomadic tribes since the revolution for two reasons. The first is their significant role in livestock raising and meat production, and the second has to do with political problems that could possibly be created by their partial settlement in urban areas. The unfavorable state of grazing lands, the imbroglio concerning ownership of those lands, and the rising prices of commodities that nomads have to procure have initiated a certain tendency towards natural settlement. In the period that elapsed between two tribal censuses in 1974 and 1985, 94,418 nomadic households settled - 89,653 in towns.

QASHQAIE TRIBE

The Turkish speaking Qashqaie tribe is the most reputed tribe in southern Iran. The Qashqaie territory extends from Abadeh and Shahreza in the Isfahan province to the Persian Gulf coast.

The tribe comprises numerous clans. The major ones are Kashkooli, Sheesh Blocki, Khalaj, Farsi Madan, Safi Khani, Rahimi, Bayat, Darreh Shuyee.

One school of thought maintains that the Qashqaies descended from the ancestors of the Turkish Khalaj clan, who lived between India and Sistan region of Iran, and then migrated to central and southern Iran. Each clan has a chief, and there was a general tribal leader who was appointed in the old days. The Qashqaie tribe has never played a decisive role in the national political developments, but it has occasionally been the source of short-lived troubles for the government.

BAKHTIYARI TRIBE

The Bakhtiyari tribe is composed of the clans living in the mountainous regions between the Chaharmahal, Fars, Khuzistan (the Taftoon Field), and Lurestan provinces.

The tribe is divided into two separate branches: Haft Gang and Chahar Gang. The former consists of 55 and the latter of 24 clans. The Arabian and Lur clans mix together in the Bakhtiari tribe. The Bakhtiari tribe is also called the Great Lur. Scholars have differing opinions on its origin. However, the opinion mostly adhered to and more extensively documented maintains the Bakhtiaris are of Kurdish origin. The Bakhtiari overlords have been influential in political developments since the era of the Safavids and the

Nader Shah. Some of their leaders helped constitutional revolutionaries conquer Tehran during the Period of Minor Despotism. That was when the Qajar king, Mohammad Ali Shah, suspended the parliament and the constitution in 1907.

Chapter 4

Current Iranian Statistics

Location: Middle East, bordering the Gulf of Oman, the Persian Gulf, and the Caspian Sea, between Iraq and Pakistan

Geographic coordinates
32 00 N, 53 00 E

Area
total: 1.648 million sq km
land: 1.636 million sq km
water: 12,000 sq km

Area Comparative
slightly larger than Alaska

Land Boundaries
total: 5,440 km
border countries: Afghanistan 936 km, Armenia 35 km, Azerbaijan-proper 432 km, Azerbaijan-Naxcivan exclave

179 km, Iraq 1,458 km, Pakistan 909 km, Turkey 499 km, Turkmenistan 992 km

Coastline
2,440 km; note - Iran also borders the Caspian Sea (740 km)

Maritime Claims
territorial sea: 12 nm
contiguous zone: 24 nm
exclusive economic zone: bilateral agreements or median lines in the Persian Gulf
continental shelf: natural prolongation

Climate
mostly arid or semiarid, subtropical along Caspian coast

Terrain
rugged, mountainous rim; high, central basin with deserts, mountains; small, discontinuous plains along both coasts

Elevation Extreams
lowest point: Caspian Sea -28 m
highest point: Kuh-e Damavand 5,671 m

Natural Resources
petroleum, natural gas, coal, chromium, copper, iron ore, lead, manganese, zinc, sulfur

Irrigated Land
76,500 sq km (2003)

Natural Hazards
periodic droughts, floods; dust storms, sandstorms; earthquakes

Enviromental Current Issues
air pollution, especially in urban areas, from vehicle emissions, refinery operations, and industrial effluents; deforestation; overgrazing; desertification; oil pollution in the Persian Gulf; wetland losses from drought; soil degradation (salination); inadequate supplies of potable water; water pollution from raw sewage and industrial waste; urbanization

Geography note:
strategic location on the Persian Gulf and Strait of Hormuz, which are vital maritime pathways for crude oil transport

Population
68,688,433 (July 2006 est.)

Age Structure
0-14 years: 26.1% (male 9,204,785/female 8,731,429)
15-64 years: 69% (male 24,133,919/female 23,245,255)
65 years and over: 4.9% (male 1,653,827/female 1,719,218) (2006 est.)

Population growth rate
1.1% (2006 est.)

Ethnic Groups
Persian 51%, Azeri 24%, Gilaki and Mazandarani 8%, Kurd 7%, Arab 3%, Lur 2%, Baloch 2%, Turkmen 2%, other 1%

Religions

Shia Muslim 89%, Sunni Muslim 9%, Zoroastrian, Jewish, Christian, and Bahai 2%

Languages

Persian and Persian dialects 58%, Turkic and Turkic dialects 26%, Kurdish 9%, Luri 2%, Balochi 1%, Arabic 1%, Turkish 1%, other 2%

Literacy

definition: age 15 and over can read and write
total population: 79.4%
male: 85.6%
female: 73% (2003 est.)

Country Name

conventional long form: Islamic Republic of Iran
conventional short form: Iran
local long form: Jomhuri-ye Eslami-ye Iran
local short form: Iran
former: Persia

Government type

theocratic republic

Capital

name: Tehran
geographic coordinates: 35 40 N, 51 26 E
time difference: UTC+3.5 (8.5 hours ahead of Washington, DC during Standard Time)

Administrative Divisions

30 provinces (ostanha, singular - ostan); Ardabil, Azarbayjan-e Gharbi, Azarbayjan-e Sharqi, Bushehr,

Chahar Mahall va Bakhtiari, Esfahan, Fars, Gilan, Golestan, Hamadan, Hormozgan, Ilam, Kerman, Kermanshah, Khorasan-e Janubi, Khorasan-e Razavi, Khorasan-e Shemali, Khuzestan, Kohgiluyeh va Buyer Ahmad, Kordestan, Lorestan, Markazi, Mazandaran, Qazvin, Qom, Semnan, Sistan va Baluchestan, Tehran, Yazd, Zanjan

Independence
1 April 1979 (Islamic Republic of Iran proclaimed)

National Holiday
Republic Day, 1 April (1979)
note: additional holidays celebrated widely in Iran include Revolution Day, 11 February (1979); Noruz (New Years Day), 21 March; Constitutional Monarchy Day, 5 August (1925); and various Islamic observances that change in accordance with the lunar-based hejira calendar

Legal System
the Constitution codifies Islamic principles of government

Executive Branch
chief of state: Supreme Leader Ali Hoseini-KHAMENEI (since 4 June 1989)
head of government: President Mahmud AHMADI-NEJAD (since 3 August 2005); First Vice President Parviz DAVUDI (since 11 September 2005)
cabinet: Council of Ministers selected by the president with legislative approval; the Supreme Leader has some control over appointments to the more sensitive ministries
note: also considered part of the Executive branch of government are three oversight bodies: 1) Assembly of Experts, a popularly elected body of 86 religious scholars

constitutionally charged with determining the succession of the Supreme Leader, reviewing his performance, and deposing him if deemed necessary; 2) Expediency Council or Council for the Discernment of Expediency is a policy advisory and implementation board consisting of permanent and temporary members representing all major government factions, some of whom are appointed by the Supreme Leader; the Council exerts supervisory authority over the executive, judicial, and legislative branches and resolves legislative issues on which the Majles and the Council of Guardians disagree; 3) Council of Guardians or Council of Guardians of the Constitution is a 12-member board of clerics and jurists serving six-year terms that determines whether proposed legislation is both constitutional and faithful to Islamic law; the Council also vets candidates for suitability and supervises national elections

elections: Supreme Leader appointed for life by the Assembly of Experts; president elected by popular vote for a four-year term (eligible for a second term); election last held 17 June 2005 with a two-candidate runoff on 24 June 2005 (next to be held in 2009)

election results: Mahmud AHMADI-NEJAD elected president; percent of vote - Mahmud AHMADI-NEJAD 62%, Ali Akbar Hashemi RAFSANJANI 36%

Legislative Branch

unicameral Islamic Consultative Assembly or Majles-e-Shura-ye-Eslami (290 seats - formerly 270 seats; members elected by popular vote to serve four-year terms)

elections: last held 20 February 2004 with a runoff held 7 in May 2004 (next to be held in February 2008)

election results: percent of vote - NA; seats by party - conservatives/Islamists 190, reformers 50, independents

43, religious minorities 5, and 2 seats unaccounted for

Judicial Branch
Supreme Court - above a special clerical court, a revolutionary court, and a special administrative court

Economy Overview
Irans economy is marked by a bloated, inefficient state sector, over reliance on the oil sector, and statist policies that create major distortions throughout. Most economic activity is controlled by the state. Private sector activity is typically small-scale - workshops, farming, and services. President Mahmud AHMADI-NEJAD has continued to follow the market reform plans of former President RAFSANJANI, with limited progress. Relatively high oil prices in recent years have enabled Iran to amass some $40 billion in foreign exchange reserves, but have not eased economic hardships such as high unemployment and inflation. The proportion of the economy devoted to the development of weapons of mass destruction remains a contentious issue with leading Western nations.

GDP(Purchasing Power Parity)
$561.6 billion (2005 est.)

GDP Per Capita
$8,300 (2005 est.)

GDP Composition by Sector
agriculture: 11.6%
industry: 42.4%
services: 46% (2005 est.)

Labor Force
23.68 million
note: shortage of skilled labor (2005 est.)

Labor Force By Occupation
agriculture: 30%
industry: 25%
services: 45% (2001 est

Unemployment Rate
11.2% (2004 est.)

Population Below Poverty line
40% (2002 est.)

Budget
revenues: $48.82 billion
expenditures: $60.4 billion; including capital expenditures of $7.6 billion (2005 est.)

Agricultural Products
wheat, rice, other grains, sugar beets, fruits, nuts, cotton; dairy products, wool; caviar

Industries
petroleum, petrochemicals, textiles, cement and other construction materials, food processing (particularly sugar refining and vegetable oil production), metal fabrication, armaments

Natural Gas Production
79 billion cu m (2003 est.)

Natural Gas Exports
3.4 billion cu m (2003 est.)

Export Commodities
petroleum 80%, chemical and petrochemical products, fruits and nuts, carpets

Export Partners
Japan 17.3%, China 11.4%, Italy 6.2%, South Africa 5.5%, South Korea 5.2%, France 4.5%, Turkey 4.5%, Taiwan 4.3%, Netherlands 4.3% (2005)

Import Commodities
industrial raw materials and intermediate goods, capital goods, foodstuffs and other consumer goods, technical services, military supplies

Import Partners
Germany 14.2%, China 8.3%, Italy 7.5%, UAE 6.7%, South Korea 6.4%, France 6.2%, Russia 5.3% (2005)

Military Branches
Islamic Republic of Iran Regular Forces (Artesh): Ground Forces, Navy, Air Force (includes air defense); Islamic Revolutionary Guard Corps (Sepah-e Pasdaran-e Enqelab-e Eslami, IRGC): Ground Forces, Navy, Air Force, Qods Force (special operations), and Basij Force (Popular Mobilization Army); Law Enforcement Forces (2004)

Military service age and obligation
18 years of age for compulsory military service; 16 years of age for volunteers; soldiers as young as 9 were recruited extensively during the Iran-Iraq War; conscript service obligation - 18 months (2004)

Manpower Available for Military Service
males age 18-49: 18,319,545
females age 18-49: 17,541,037 (2005 est.)

Manpower Fit for Military Service
males age 18-49: 15,665,725
females age 18-49: 15,005,597 (2005 est.)

Manpower reaching military age annually
males age 18-49: 862,056
females age 18-49: 808,044 (2005 est.)

Military Expenditure Dollar figure
$4.3 billion (2003 est.)

Illicit Drugs
despite substantial interdiction efforts, Iran remains a key transshipment point for Southwest Asian heroin to Europe; domestic narcotics consumption remains a persistent problem and according to official Iranian statistics there are at least 2 million drug users in the country; lacks anti-money-laundering laws

Chapter 5

Regional Shias in percentage

The Shia population in each of the following countries is growing, and will soon reach a sizable portion, and combined together will create a dominant force in Asia and the Middle East region. The world needs to keep an eye on the Iranian proxy.

Following countries and their Shia population in percentage

Country	Shia in percent
Iran	95% Shia
Iraq	63% Shia
Pakistan	30% Shia
Afghanistan	15% Shia
Kazakhstan	8% Shia
Uzbekistan	3% Shia
Turkmenistan	2% Shia

Yemen	42% Shia
Qatar	3% Shia
Oman	5% Shia
Bahrain	70% Shia
Kuwait	3% Shia
Saudi Arabia	18% Shia
Syria	16% Allawi or declared Shia by Clerics
Lebonan	20% Shia
Turkey	3% Shia
Azerbaijan	61% Shi'aithna offshoot of shia sect

By a recent U.S. intelligence review, Iran may be 5 to 10 years away from a bomb. I strongly feel Iran is a lot closer than the estimates and in my opinion under 5 years. Irans goals are to unify the Shia populations of the region and eventually creating an Empire under a Shia Cresent. A Nuclear Iran will be very capable of achieving this goal within two decades at the most, enjoining the various Shia populations and gaining control of the Middle East. Everyone saw what the Iranian proxy Hezbollah did during the recent clash in July of 2006, and this is an Iranian influence that does not have Nuclear capability yet. The daily suicide bombing in Iraq proves my point that Iranian regime is working very hard to destabilize the region to it own advantage, so eventually it can gain regional control. The overthrow of Saddam Husain was in total favor of Iran, our policy makers saw Saddams removal as checkmating Iran, it has proven quite the opposite the Clerics have gotten one step closer to their goal. When it comes down to it the newly elected Shia government in Iraq will go along with the Mullahs or the Ayatollahs of the region due to their influence over the common public. The world would be facing a dangerous threat if we allow the Iranian regime to have Nuclear weapons. Pulling out of Iraq could prove to be a monumental mistake at this time, we must face the facts that we are there long term, in order to secure our vital interest in the region.

Iran goes nuclear, she has a deterrent to intimidation. U.S. freedom of action in the Persian Gulf will come to an end. We would have to behave as gingerly with the mullahs as we do with Kim Jong Il. For the Israelis, an Iranian bomb would have the same impact as Stalins explosion of a bomb had on us in 1949. Israels invulnerability would come to an end. She would enter the world of Mutual Assured Destruction, like the one we had to live in during the Cold War. Thus, for Israel, the sooner the Americans pulverize Irans infant nuclear facilities, the better.

Chapter 6

President Mahmood Ahmadi Nejad

D r. Mahmoud Ahmadi Nejad was born in 1956 in the village of Aradan in the city of Garmsar. He moved and stayed in Tehran together with his family while he was still one-year old and completed his primary as well as his low and high secondary education there. In 1975, he successfully passed the university entrance exam with high marks and started his academic studies on the subject of civil engineering in the Science and Technology University in Tehran.

In 1986, he continued his studies at MS level in the same university. In 1989, he became a member of the Board of Civil Engineering Faculty of the Science and Technology University. In 1997, he managed to obtain his Ph.D. on transportation engineering and planning from the Science and Technology University.

Dr. Ahmadi Nejad is familiar with English language. During the years when he was teaching in the university, he wrote many scientific papers and engaged in scientific research in various fields. During the same period, he also supervised the theses of tens of students at MS and Ph.D. levels on different subjects of civil engineering, road and transportation as well as construction management.

While still a student, Dr. Ahmadi Nejad engaged in political activities by attending religious and political meetings before the Islamic Revolution. With the victory of the Islamic Revolution, he became a founder and also a member of the Islamic Association of Students in the Science and Technology University. During the war imposed on Iran, Dr. Ahmadi Nejad was actively present as a member of the volunteer forces (Basij) in different parts and divisions of the battlefronts particularly in the war engineering division until the end of the war.

Dr. Ahmadi Nejad is married and has three children-two sons and one daughter.

Career Background:

- Governor of Maku
- Governor of Khoy
- Advisor to the Governor General of Kordistan Province
- Advisor for cultural affairs to the Minister of Culture and Higher Education (1993)
- Governor General of Ardabil Province (1993-1997)
- Member of the Board of Civil Engineering Faculty of the Science and Technology University (since 1989 till present date)
- Tehran Mayor (2003-2005)
- He was elected by the Iranian people as the

President during the 9th presidential election on June 24, 2005. In addition to his academic and scientific pursuits as well as his executive positions, Dr. Ahmadi Nejad has engaged in the following careers and activities as well

• Journalism; writing various political, social, cultural and economic articles,

• In the same career, he also held the position of managing director of Hamshahri newspaper and launched various affiliated periodicals including Neighborhood Hamshahri published and distributed in 22 areas of the city of Tehran, Hamshahri for Passengers, Diplomatic Hamshahri, Youth Hamshahri, Monthly Hamshahri and also extra pages attached to the Hamshahri newspaper for thinkers, students, etc.

• Founding and work ing as a member of Iran Tunnel Society,

• Working as a member of Iran Civil Engineering Society,

• Working as a member of the first central council of the Islamic Association of Students in the Science and Technology University,

• Working as a member of the first central council of the Union of Islamic Associations of University and Higher Education Institutes in Iran.

Presidential campaign

Ahmadinejad generally sent mixed signals about his plans for his presidency, which some US-based analysts considered to have been designed to attract both religious conservatives and the lower economic classes his campaign motto was, Its possible and we can do it.

In his presidential campaign, Ahmadinejad took a populist approach, with emphasis on his own modest life, and had compared himself with Mohammad Ali Rajai, the second president of Iran—a claim that raised objections from Rajais family. Ahmadinejad claims he plans to create an exemplary government for the people of the world in Iran. He is a self-described principlist; that is, acting politically based on Islamic and revolutionary principles. One of his goals is putting the petroleum income on peoples tables, referring to Irans oil profits being distributed among the poor.

Ahmadinejad was the only presidential candidate who spoke out against future relations with the United States. Also, in an interview with Islamic Republic of Iran Broadcasting a few days before the elections, Ahmadinejad accused the United Nations of being one-sided, stacked against the world of Islam. He has openly opposed the veto power given to the five permanent members of the UN Security Council. In the same interview, he stated, It is not just for a few states to sit and veto global approvals. Should such a privilege continue to exist, the Muslim world with a population of nearly 1.5 billion should be extended the same privilege. In addition, he has defended Irans nuclear program and has accused a few arrogant powers of attempting to limit Irans industrial and technological development in this and other fields.

After his election he proclaimed, Thanks to the blood of the martyrs, a new Islamic revolution has arisen and the Islamic revolution of 1384 [the current Iranian year] will, if God wills, cut off the roots of injustice in the world. He said, that the wave of the Islamic revolution would soon reach the entire world.

During his campaign for the second round, he said, We

didnt participate in the revolution for turn-by-turn government....This revolution tries to reach a world-wide government. Also he has mentioned that he has an extended program on fighting terrorism in order to improve foreign relations and has called for greater ties with Irans neighbours and ending visa requirements between states in the region, saying that people should visit anywhere they wish freely. People should have freedom in their pilgrimages and tours.As confirmed by Ahmadinejad, Ayatollah Mohammad Taghi Mesbah Yazdi, a senior cleric from Qom, is President Ahmadinejads ideological mentor and spiritual guide. Mesbah is the founder of Haghani School of thought in Iran. He and his team strongly supported Ahmadinejads campaign during presidential election in 2005.

Ahmadinejad was appointed the President of Iran on August 3, 2005, receiving the approval of Supreme Leader Ayatollah Khamenei. During the inauguration ceremony he kissed Khameneis hand in demonstration of his loyalty to him. The act caused a stir in the national media as he is the first Iranian president to kiss Khameneis hand and the second Iranian president (after Mohammad Ali Rajai) to kiss a Supreme Leaders hand. Khameneis eldest son Mujtaba was Ahmadinejads campaign manager during the election, and Ahmadinejad was widely perceived at the time of his election to be Khameneis protégé. In a speech in 2006 Khamenei said: This government is the most favorite government of Iran in 100 years.

In the first announcement after his presidency, Ahmadinejad asked the public servants not to post his photographs and pictures in governmental offices and use the pictures and photos of Khomeini and Khamenei only. Ahmadinejad completed the requisite inaugural ceremonies on August 6, when he took a vow before the Majlis to protect Irans national institutions: Shia Islam, the Islamic Republic, and the Constitution of Iran. Mohammad Reza Aref, Khatamis First Vice President, had been Acting President during the period of inaugural ceremonies.

Cabinet

Ahmadinejad was required to introduce his suggested ministers to Majlis for a vote of approval in fifteen days, after which Majlis would have one week to decide about the ministers. It was mentioned by Masoud Zaribafan, Ahmadinejads campaign manager, that Ahmadinejad would probably introduce his cabinet on the same day of his vow, which did not happen, but the list was finally sent to the Majlis on August 14. The Majlis were set to vote on the suggested ministers by August 21.

The parliament had held a private meeting on August 5, when Ahmadinejad presented a shortlist of three or four candidates for each ministry, to know the opinion of Majlis about his candidates. A news website close to Ahmadinejad published a partial list of Ahmadinejads decisions based on the feedback, which was updated and changed a few times. The final list was officially sent to the Majlis on August 14, 2005.

After a few days of heavy discussions in Majlis, which started on August 21, 2005, Ahmadinejads cabinet was voted for on August 24, 2005, and became the first cabinet since the Iranian revolution in not winning a complete vote of approval. Four candidates, for the ministries of Cooperatives, Education, Petroleum, and Welfare and Social Security, all previous colleagues of Ahmadinejad in the Municipality of Tehran, were voted down, with the other candidates becoming ministers.

Nuclear visions

Ahmadinejad has been a vocal supporter of Irans nuclear program. On January 11, 2006, Ahmadinejad announced that Iran would have *peaceful nuclear technology* very soon. He also emphasized that building the nuclear bomb is not the policy of his government. He reportedly said that there was no such policy and that such a policy was illegal and against our religion.

He also added at a January 2006 conference in Tehran that a nation that had culture, logic and civilisation would not need nuclear weapons, but that countries which sought nuclear weapons were those which wanted to solve all problems by the use of force.

Ahmadinejad reportedly invited all countries to participate in Irans nuclear project He turned down an offer by Russian president Vladimir Putin to process uranium in order for Iran to use it. In April 2006, Ahmadinejad announced that Iran had successfully refined uranium to a stage suitable for the nuclear fuel cycle. In a speech to students and academics in Mashad, he was quoted saying that Irans conditions had changed completely as it became a nuclear state and could talk to other states from that stand.

On April 13, 2006, Iranian news agency IRNA quoted Ahmadinejad as saying that the peaceful Iranian nuclear technology would not pose a threat to any party because we want peace and stability and we will not cause injustice to anyone and at the same time we will not submit to injustice.

However, the office of the Iranian President is not responsible for nuclear policy. It is instead set by the Supreme National Security Council. The council includes representatives appointed by the Supreme Leader, military officials and members of the executive, judicial and legislative branches of government and reports directly to

Supreme Leader Ali Khamenei, who reportedly issued a fatwa against nuclear weapons in 2005.

United States - Iran relations

On May 8, 2006, Ahmadinejad sent a personal letter to United States President George Bush to propose new ways to end Irans nuclear dispute. U.S. Secretary of State Condoleezza Rice and National Security Adviser Stephen Hadley both reviewed the letter and dismissed it as a negotiating ploy and publicity stunt that did not address U.S. concerns about Irans nuclear program. The letter was meant to be an invitation to Islam and took a broad, historical look at the U.S.-Iranian relationship. It was the first contact between both governments since April 9, 1980. Ahmadinejad denied that his aim was to provoke the United States.

On August 8, 2006, he gave a television interview to Mike Wallace, a correspondent for 60 Minutes. It was his first interview for U.S. media after 6 months.

On August 29, 2006, he invited George W. Bush to an open televised debate on his plan to have a peaceful nuclear program in place. The invitation was promptly rejected by the White house.

Iran-Russia relations

Ahmadinejad has moved to strengthen relations with Russia, setting up an office expressly dedicated to the purpose in October 2005. He has worked with Vladimir Putin on the nuclear issue, and both Putin and Ahmadinejad have expressed a desire for more mutual cooperation on issues involving the Caspian Sea. However, Western intelligence officials recently accused Ahmadinejad of sanctioning the training and funding of Chechen rebels, who are fighting against Russia, inside Iran

Controversies surrounding Ahmadi Nejad

On June 29, 2005, shortly after Mahmoud Ahmadinejad won the Iranian presidential election, several major western news outlets publicized various allegations against him. These include charges that he participated heavily in the 1979-1981 Iran Hostage Crisis, assassinations of Kurdish politicians in Austria, support of or involvement in terrorist activities, torture, interrogation and executions of political prisoners in the Evin prison in Tehran.

Ahmadinejad and his political supporters have denied these allegations. Additionally, a number of Ahmadinejads political opponents in Iran have specifically denied allegations of his participation in the Iran Hostage Crisis. The Iranian government stated that the allegations circulating against Ahmadinejad in the Western media are merely part of a smear campaign orchestrated by the United States and what Iranian officials have referred to as Zionist media, directed against Ahmadinejad in specific and Iran in general.

In July of 2005, US President George W. Bush declared that these charges were serious and must be investigated; as of the end of November 2005, the US government claims that it continues investigating the charges. As of July of 2005, no independent commission has surfaced to investigate these charges and pronounce its findings.

From before the second round of the election, in late July 2005, there have also been allegations of political corruption from Ahmadinejads political opponents inside Iran, especially his opponents in the reformist party.

Iran-Israel relations

In October 2005 Ahmadinejad gave a speech that contained antagonistic statements about Israel. According to widely published translations, he agreed with a statement he attributed to Ayatollah Khomeini that the *occupying regime* had to be removed, and referred to Israel as a disgraceful stain [on] the Islamic world that would be eliminated.

Ahmadinejads comments were condemned by major Western governments, the European Union, Russia, the United Nations Security Council and UN Secretary General Kofi Annan. Egyptian, Turkish and Palestinian leaders also expressed displeasure over Ahmadinejads remark. Canadas then Prime Minister Paul Martin said, this threat to Israels existence, this call for genocide coupled with Irans obvious nuclear ambitions is a matter that the world cannot ignore.

The translation of his statement has been disputed. At a news conference on January 14, 2006, Ahmadinejad claimed regarding the October speech There is no new policy, they created a lot of hue and cry over that. In June, 2006 Guardian columnist and foreign correspondent Jonathan Steele cited several Farsi speakers and translators who state that the phrase in question is more accurately translated as eliminated or wiped off or wiped away from the page of time or the pages of history, rather than wiped off the map. Reviewing the controversy over the translation, New York Times deputy foreign editor Ethan Bronner observed that all official translations of the comments, including the foreign ministry and presidents office, refer to wiping Israel away.

Ahmadinejad also compared Israels actions in the 2006 Israel-Lebanon conflict to Adolf Hitlers actions during WWII saying that Hitler sought pretexts to attack other nations and that the Zionist regime is seeking baseless pretexts to invade Islamic countries and right now it is justifying its attacks with groundless excuses.

On August 8, 2006, he gave a television interview to Mike Wallace, a correspondent for 60 Minutes, in which he talked about what he views as Israels culpability for Lebanese suffering and the moral justification for Hezbollahs missile attacks. Later on in the interview Ahmadinejad was pressed on his views regarding the state of Israel, and asked to explain his previous statements questioning its right to exist, and suggesting that it should be relocated to Europe, since Europeans should have been forced to bear primary culpability for the Holocaust.

Chapter 7

Nuclear program of Iran

Originally started under the Shah of Iran in the 1950s, with the help of the United States, the **Iranian nuclear program** is an effort by Iran to develop nuclear technology. After the 1979 revolution, the program was temporarily disbanded. It was soon resumed, albeit with less Western assistance than the pre-revolution era. Irans current nuclear program consists of several research sites, a uranium mine, a nuclear reactor, and uranium processing facilities that include a uranium enrichment plant. The Iranian government asserts that the programs only goal is to develop the capacity for peaceful nuclear power generation, and plans to generate 6000MW of electricity with nuclear power plants by 2010. As of 2006 nuclear power does not contribute to the Iranian energy grid.

U.S.-Iran nuclear co-operation in the 1950s and 60s

The foundations for Irans nuclear program were laid during the Cold War, in the late 1950s under auspices of the U.S. within the framework of bilateral agreements between the U.S. and Iran. A civil nuclear co-operation program was signed as soon as 1957 with the U.S. under the Atoms for Peace program. The Shah Mohammad Reza Pahlavi was ruling Iran at that time, and after Mohammed Mossadeghs 1953 overthrow supported by the CIA, the regime appeared sufficiently stable and friendly to the West that nuclear proliferation would not become a threat.

In 1959 the Tehran Nuclear Research Center (TNRC) was established, run by the Atomic Energy Organization of Iran (AEOI). The TNRC was equipped with a U.S.-supplied 5-megawatt nuclear research reactor, operational from 1967 and fuelled with highly enriched uranium. Iran signed the Nuclear Non-Proliferation Treaty (NPT) in 1968 and ratified it in 1970. With the establishment of Irans atomic agency and the NPT in place, plans were drawn by the Shah Mohammad Pahlavi to construct up to 23 nuclear power stations across the country together with the USA by the year 2000.

U.S.-Iran nuclear co-operation in the 1970s

In March 1974, the Shah envisioned a time when the worlds oil supply would run out, and declared, Petroleum is a noble material, much too valuable to burn... We envision producing, as soon as possible, 23 000 megawatts of electricity using nuclear plants. Bushehr would be the first plant, and would supply energy to the inland city of Shiraz. In 1975, the Bonn firm Kraftwerk Union AG, a joint venture of Siemens AG and AEG Telefunken, signed a contract worth $4 to $6 billion to build the pressurized water reactor nuclear power plant. Construction of the two 1,196 MWe nuclear generating units was subcontracted to ThyssenKrupp, and was to have been completed in 1981.

By 1975 U.S. Secretary of State, Henry Kissinger, had signed *National Security Decision Memorandum 292*, titled **U.S.-Iran Nuclear Co-operation**, which laid out the details of the sale of nuclear energy equipment to Iran projected to bring U.S. corporations more than $6 billion in revenue. At the time, Iran was pumping as much as 6 million barrels (950,000 m^3) of oil a day, compared with about 4 million barrels (640,000 m^3) daily today.

President Gerald Ford hesitantly signed a directive in 1976 offering Tehran the opportunity to buy and operate a U.S.-built reprocessing facility for extracting plutonium from nuclear reactor fuel. The deal was for a complete nuclear fuel cycle, with all the proliferation risks that would entail. The Ford strategy paper said the introduction of nuclear power will both provide for the growing needs of Irans economy and free remaining oil reserves for export or conversion to petrochemicals.

President Fords team endorsed Iranian plans to build a massive nuclear energy industry, but also worked hard to complete a multibillion-dollar deal that would have given Tehran control of large quantities of plutonium and enriched uranium -- the two pathways to a nuclear bomb. Iran, a U.S. ally then, had deep pockets and close ties to Washington. U.S. companies, including Westinghouse and General Electric, scrambled to do business there.

In an interview for a newspaper article on March 27, 2005, Henry Kissinger said, I dont think the issue of proliferation came up.

Until the change of administration in 1977, Dick

Cheney, U.S. Secretary of Defense Donald Rumsfeld, and Paul Wolfowitz, some of the strongest opponents of Irans nuclear program today, were all heavily involved in promoting an Iranian nuclear program that could extract plutonium from nuclear reactor fuel for use in nuclear weapons. In fairness, it must be noted that Iran was an ally of the United States at the time.

After the 1979 Revolution

After the 1979 Revolution, Iran informed the International Atomic Energy Agency (IAEA) of its plans to restart its nuclear program using indigenously-made nuclear fuel, and in 1983 the IAEA even planned to provide assistance to Iran under its Technical Assistance Program to produce enriched uranium. An IAEA report stated clearly that its aim was to contribute to the formation of local expertise and manpower needed to sustain an ambitious program in the field of nuclear power reactor technology and fuel cycle technology. However, the IAEA was forced to terminate the program under U.S. pressure. The revolution was a turning point in terms of foreign cooperation on nuclear technology.

Another result of the 1979 Revolution was Frances refusal to give any enriched uranium to Iran after 1979. Iran also didnt get back its investment from Eurodif. The joint stock company Eurodif was formed in 1973 by France, Belgium, Spain and Sweden. In 1975 Swedens 10% share in Eurodif went to Iran as a result of an arrangement between France and Iran. The French government subsidiary company Cogéma and the Iranian Government established the Sofidif (*Société franco–iranienne pour lenrichissement de luranium par diffusion gazeuse*) enterprise with 60% and 40% shares, respectively. In turn, Sofidif acquired a 25% share in EURODIF, which gave Iran its 10% share of Eurodif. Reza Shah Pahlavi lent 1 billion dollars (and another 180 million dollars in 1977) for the construction of the Eurodif factory, to have the right of buying 10% of the production of the site.

The U.S. was also paid to deliver new fuel and upgrade its power in accordance with a contract signed before the revolution. The U.S. delivered neither the fuel nor returned the billions of dollars payment it had received. Germany was paid for in full, billions of dollars for the two nuclear facilities in Bushehr, but after three decades, Germany has also refused to export any equipment or refund the money. Irans government suspended its payments and tried refunding the loan by making pressure on France by handling militant groups, including the Hezbollah who took French citizens hostage in the 1980s. In 1982, president François Mitterrand refused to give any uranium to Iran, which also claimed the $1 billion debt. In 1986, Eurodif manager Georges Besse was assassinated; the act was allegedly claimed by left-wing militants from Action Directe. However, they denied any responsibility during their trial. In their investigation *La République atomique, France-Iran le pacte nucléaire*, David Carr-Brown and Dominique Lorentz pointed out toward the Iranian intelligence services responsibility. More importantly, they also showed how the French hostage scandal was connected with the Iranian blackmail. Finally an agreement was found in 1991: France refunded more than 1.6 billion dollars. Iran remained shareholder of Eurodif via Sofidif, a Franco-Iranian consortium shareholder to 25% of Eurodif. However, Iran abstained itself from asking for the produced uranium.

Kraftwerk Union, the joint venture of Siemens AG and

AEG Telefunken who had signed a contract with Iran in 1975, fully withdrew from the Bushehr nuclear project in July 1979, after work stopped in January 1979, with one reactor 50% complete, and the other reactor 85% complete. They said they based their action on Irans non-payment of $450 million in overdue payments. The company had received $2.5 billion of the total contract. Their cancellation came after certainty that the Iranian government would unilaterally terminate the contract themselves, following the revolution, which paralyzed Irans economy and led to a crisis in Irans relations with the West. The French company Framatome, a subsidiary of Areva, also withdrew itself.

In 1984, Kraftwerk Union did a preliminary assessment to see if it could resume work on the project, but declined to do so while the Iran-Iraq War continued. In April of that year, the U.S. State Department said, We believe it would take at least two to three years to complete construction of the reactors at Bushehr. The spokesperson also said that the light water power reactors at Bushehr are not particularly well-suited for a weapons program. The spokesman went on to say, In addition, we have no evidence of Iranian construction of other facilities that would be necessary to separate plutonium from spent reactor fuel.

The Bushehr reactors were then damaged by multiple Iraqi air strikes between March 24, 1984 to 1988 and work on the nuclear program came to a standstill. In 1990, Iran began to look outwards towards partners for its nuclear program; however, due to a radically different political climate and punitive U.S. economic sanctions, few candidates existed.

According to IAEA spokesperson Melissa Fleming, IAEA inspectors visited Irans uranium mines in 1992.

In 1995, Iran signed a contract with Russia to resume

work on the partially complete Bushehr plant, installing into the existing Bushehr I building a 915MWe VVER-1000 pressurized water reactor, with completion expected in 2007. There are no current plans to complete Bushehr II reactor.

In 1996, the U.S. tried, without success, to block China from selling to Tehran a conversion plant. China also provided Iran with gas needed to test the uranium enrichment process

On August 14, 2002, Alireza Jafarzadeh, a prominent Iranian dissident, revealed the existence of two unknown nuclear sites, a uranium enrichment facility in Natanz (part of which is underground) and a heavy water facility in Arak.

Though it is often claimed that Iran had concealed its enrichment programme from the IAEA in violation of the NPT until it was caught cheating in 2002, the fact is that Iran was not obliged to inform the Agency about those facilities at the time since according to Irans safeguards agreement with the IAEA in force at the time, Iran is not required to allow IAEA inspections of a new nuclear facility until six months before nuclear material is introduced into it. In fact, it was not even required to inform the IAEA of their existence until then, a point conceded by Britain at the March 2003 Board of Governors meeting. This `six months clause was a standard part of all IAEA safeguards agreements. Nonetheless, Iran allowed intrusive inspections of the facilities by the IAEA pursuant to the Additional Protocol, and the IAEA concluded that the facilities were not related to any secret nuclear weapons program. (Iran and the invention of a nuclear crisis by Siddharth Varadarajan,

On November 14, 2004, Irans chief nuclear negotiator announced a voluntary and temporary suspension of its uranium enrichment program (enrichment is not a violation of the NPT) after pressure from the United Kingdom, France, and Germany acting on behalf of the European Union (EU) (known in this context as the *EU-3*). The measure was said at the time to be a confidence-building measure, to continue for some reasonable period of time, six months being mentioned as a reference. On November 24, Iran sought to amend the terms of its agreement with the EU to exclude a handful of the equipment from this deal for research work. This request was dropped four days later.

On August 8 and August 10, 2005, the Iranian government resumed its conversion of uranium at the Isfahan facility, coming only five days after the election of Mahmoud Ahmadinejad, allegedly with continued suspension of enrichment activities. This led to (on September 19, 2005) the European Union pressuring the IAEA to bring Irans nuclear program before the United Nations Security Council.

In January 2006, James Risen, a New York Times reporter, alleged in his book *State of War* that in February 2000, a U.S. covert operation - code-named *Operation Merlin* - had backfired. It originally aimed to provide Iran with a flawed design for building a nuclear weapon, in order to delay the alleged Iranian nuclear weapons program. Instead, the plan may have accelerated Irans nuclear program by providing useful information, once the flaws were identified

On February 4, 2006, the 35 member Board of Governors of the IAEA voted 27-3 (with five abstentions: Algeria, Belarus, Indonesia, Libya and South Africa) to report Iran to the UN Security Council. The measure was sponsored by the United Kingdom, France and Germany, and it was backed by the United States. Two permanent council members, Russia and China, agreed to referral only on condition that the council take no action before March. The three members who voted against referral were Venezuela, Syria and Cuba.

On April 11, 2006, Iranian President Mahmoud Ahmadinejad announced that Iran had successfully enriched uranium. President Ahmadinejad made the announcement in a televised address from the northeastern city of Mashhad, where he said I am officially announcing that Iran joined the group of those countries which have nuclear technology. The uranium was enriched to 3.5% using over a hundred centrifuges. At this level, it could be used in a nuclear reactor if enough of it was made; uranium for a nuclear bomb would require around 90% enrichment and many thousands of centrifuges to be built and operated.

President George W. Bush insisted August 31, 2006 that there must be consequences for Irans defiance of demands that it stop enriching uranium. He said the world now faces a grave threat from the radical regime in Iran, demonstrated by the war between Iranian-backed [(Hezbollah]] militants and Israel. The U.N.s nuclear watchdog agency issued a report saying Iran has not suspended its uranium enrichment activities, a United Nations official told. The report by the International Atomic Energy Agency opens the way for U.N. Security Council sanctions against Tehran. Facing a Security Council deadline to stop its uranium enrichment activities, Iran has left little doubt it will defy the West and continue its nuclear program. Iranian President Mahmoud Ahmadinejad told a crowd August 31, 2006 in a televised speech in the northwestern Iranian city of Orumiyeh. In front of his strongest supporters in one of his provincial power bases, the Iranian leader attacked what he called intimidation by the United Nations, which he said was led by the United States. Ahmadinejad criticized a White House rebuff of his offer for a televised debate with President Bush. They say they support dialogue and the free flow of information, he said. But when debate was proposed, they avoided and opposed it. Ahmadinejad said that sanctions cannot dissuade Iranians from their decision to make progress, according to Irans state-run IRNA news agency. On the contrary, many of our successes, including access to the nuclear fuel cycle and producing of heavy water, have been achieved under sanctions. Iran has been under IAEA investigation since 2003, with inspectors turning up evidence of clandestine plutonium experiments, black-market centrifuge purchases and military links to what Iran says is a civilian nuclear program.

John Bolton, the U.S. ambassador to the United Nations, said August 31, 2006 he expected action to impose sanctions to begin immediately after the deadline passes, with meetings of high-level officials in the coming days, followed by negotiations on the language of the sanctions resolution. Bolton said that when the deadline passes a little flag will go up. In terms of what happens afterward, at that point, if they have not suspended all uranium enrichment activities, they will not be in compliance with the resolution, he said. And at that point, the steps that the foreign ministers have agreed upon previously ... we would begin to talk about how to implement those steps. The five permanent members of the Security Council, plus Germany, previously offered Iran a package of incentives aimed at getting the Islamic republic to restart negotiations, but Iran refused to halt its nuclear activities first. Incentives included offers to improve Irans access to the international economy through participation in groups such as the World Trade Organization and to modernize its telecommunications industry. The incentives also mentioned the possibility of lifting restrictions on U.S. and European manufacturers wanting to export civil aircraft to Iran. And a proposed long-term agreement accompanying the incentives offered a fresh start in negotiations.

The Iranian Point of View

Iran says that nuclear power is necessary for a booming population and rapidly industrialising nation. It points to the fact that Irans population has more than doubled in 20 years, the country regularly imports gasoline and electricity, and that burning fossil fuel in large amounts harms Irans environment drastically

Additionally, Iran wishes to diversify its sources of energy, which will eventually become depleted. Irans oil reserves are currently estimated at 133 gigabarrels, at a current pumping rate of 1.5-1.8 gigabarrels per year. This is only enough oil to last the next 74-89 years assuming pumping rates are steady and additional reserves are not found. In taking a stance that the Shah expressed decades ago, Iranians feel its valuable oil should be used for high value products, not simple electricity generation. (Quote from the Shah in 1974 Petroleum is a noble material, much too valuable to burn... We envision producing, as soon as possible, 23 000 megawatts of electricity using nuclear plants.) Iran also raises financial questions, claiming that developing the excess capacity in its oil industry would cost it $40 billion, let alone pay for the power plants. Harnessing nuclear power costs a fraction of this, considering Iran has supplies of accessible uranium ore.

Dr. William O. Beeman, Brown Universitys Middle East Studies program professor, who spent years in Iran, says that the Iranian nuclear issue is a unified point of their political discussion:

The Iranian side of the discourse is that they want to be known and seen as a modern, developing state with a modern, developing industrial base. The history of relations between Iran and the West for the last hundred years has included Irans developing various kinds of industrial and technological advances to prove to themselves--and to attempt to prove to the world--that they are, in fact, that kind of country.

The nuclear-power issue is exactly that. When Iranians talk about it, and talk about the United States, they say, The United States is trying to repress us; theyre trying to keep us down and keep us backward, make us a second-class nation. And we have the ability to develop a nuclear industry, and were being told were not good enough, or we cant. And this makes people furious--not just the clerical establishment, but this makes the person on the street, even 16- and 17-year-olds, absolutely boil with anger. It is such an emotional issue that absolutely no politician could ever back down on this question.

Dr. William O. Beeman also points out that the United States policy towards the Iranian nuclear program has shifted greatly from the 1970s:

White House staff members, who are trying to prevent Iran from developing its own nuclear energy capacity and who refuse to take military action against Iran off the table, have conveniently forgotten that the United States was the midwife to the Iranian nuclear program 30 years ago.

The Iran-based newspaper Baztab recently reported that the United States had provided 5 kg of 19.7% enriched uranium to Iran before the revolution. The 1979 revolution marked a turning point in US policy, justified by a government that was becoming more fundamentalist and anti-Western. This previous involvement provided foreign countries the opportunity to keep tabs on the progress of the Iranian program, but since 1979 foreign involvement in the program is virtually null.

After the 1979 Iranian Revolution, Iran informed the International Atomic Energy Agency (IAEA) of its plans to restart its nuclear program using indigenously-made nuclear fuel, and in 1983 the IAEA even planned to provide assistance to Iran under its Technical Assistance Program to produce enriched uranium. An IAEA report stated clearly that its aim was to contribute to the formation of local expertise and manpower needed to sustain an ambitious program in the field of nuclear power reactor technology and fuel cycle technology. However, the IAEA was forced to terminate the program under U.S. pressure.

Iran also believes it has a legal right to enrich uranium for peaceful purposes under the Nuclear Non-Proliferation Treaty, a right which in 2005 the U.S. and the EU-3 began to assert had been forfeited by a clandestine nuclear program that supposedly came to light in 2002. In fact, Irans enrichment program was openly discussed on national radio, and IAEA inspectors had even visited Irans uranium mines. Iranian politicians compare its treatment as a signatory to the NPT with three nations that have not signed the NPT: Israel, India, and Pakistan. Each of these nations developed an indigenous nuclear weapons capability: Israel by 1968 India by 1974 and Pakistan by 1990

Nuclear facilities in Iran

Anarak

Anarak has a waste storage site, near Yazd.

Arak

Arak was one of the two sites exposed by <u>Alireza Jafarzadeh</u> in 2002. Iran is constructing a heavy water moderated reactor at this location, which should be ready for commissioning in 2014. In August 2006, Iran announced inaugrated the Arak plant for the production of heavy water.

Ardekan

Construction of a nuclear fuel site at Adekan is reportedly scheduled to be finished in mid-2005.

Bonab

The Atomic Energy Research Center at Bonab is investigating the applications of nuclear technology in agriculture. It is run by the AEOI.

Bushehr

The Bushehr Nuclear Power Facility is located 17 kilometers south of the city of Bushehr (also known as Bushire), between the fishing villages of Halileh and Bandargeh along the Persian Gulf.

The facility was the idea of the Shah Mohammad Reza Pahlavi, who envisioned a time when the worlds oil supply would run out. He wanted a national electrical grid powered by clean nuclear power plants. Bushehr would be the first plant, and would supply energy to the inland city of Shiraz. In August 1974, the Shah said, Petroleum is a noble material, much too valuable to burn... We envision producing, as soon as possible, 23 000 megawatts of electricity using nuclear plants.

In 1975, the Bonn firm Kraftwerk Union AG, a joint venture of Siemens AG and AEG Telefunken, signed a contract worth $4 to $6 billion to build the pressurized water reactor nuclear power plant. Construction of the two 1,196 MWe nuclear generating units was subcontracted to ThyssenKrupp AG, and was to have been completed in 1981.

Kraftwerk Union was eager to work with the Iranian government because, as spokesman Joachim Hospe said in 1976, To fully exploit our nuclear power plant capacity, we have to land at least three contracts a year for delivery abroad. The market here is about saturated, and the United States has cornered most of the rest of Europe, so we have to concentrate on the third world.

Kraftwerk Union fully withdrew from the Bushehr nuclear project in July 1979, after work stopped in January 1979, with one reactor 50% complete, and the other reactor 85% complete. They said they based their action on Irans non-payment of $450 million in overdue payments. The company had received $2.5 billion of the total contract. Their cancellation came after certainty that the Iranian government would unilaterally terminate the contract themselves, following the 1979 Iranian Revolution, which paralyzed Irans economy and led to a crisis in Irans relations with the West.

In 1984, Kraftwerk Union did a preliminary assessment to see if it could resume work on the project, but declined to do so while the Iran-Iraq war continued. In April of that year, the U.S. State Department said, We believe it would take at least two to three years to complete construction of the reactors at Bushehr. The spokesperson also said that the light water power reactors at Bushehr are not particularly well-suited for a weapons program. The spokesman went on to say, In addition, we have no evidence of Iranian construction of other facilities that would be necessary to separate plutonium from spent reactor fuel.

The reactors were then damaged by multiple Iraqi air strikes from 1984 to 1988. Shortly afterwards Iraq invaded Iran and the nuclear program was stopped until the end of the war.

In 1990, Iran began to look outwards towards partners for its nuclear program; however, due to a radically different political climate and punitive U.S. economic sanctions, few candidates existed.

In 1995 Iran signed a contract with Russia to resume work on the partially complete Bushehr plant, installing into the existing Bushehr I building a 915MWe VVER-1000 pressurized water reactor, with completion expected in 2007. The Russian state-controlled company Atomstroyexport (Atomic Construction Export), an arm of Russias atomic energy ministry, MinAtom, is constructing the plant. There are no current plans to complete Bushehr II reactor

Chalus

In 1995 Iranian exiles living in Europe claimed Iran was building a secret facility for building nuclear weapons in a mountain 20 kilometres from the town of Chalus. In October 2003 <u>Mohamed ElBaradei</u> announced that *In terms of inspections, so far, we have been allowed to visit those sites to which we have requested access.* It therefore appears the allegations about the Chalus site were unfounded

Isfahan

The Nuclear Technology Center of Isfahan is a nuclear research facility that currently operates four small nuclear research reactors, all supplied by China. It is run by the AEOI.

The Uranium Conversion Facility at Isfahan converts <u>yellowcake</u> into <u>uranium hexafluoride</u>. As of late October 2004, the site is 70% operational with 21 of 24 workshops completed. There is also a Zirconium Production Plant (ZPP) located nearby that produces the necessary ingredients and alloys for nuclear reactors.

Karaj

The Center for Agricultural Research and Nuclear Medicine at Hashtgerd was established in 1991 and is run by the AEOI.

Lashkar Abad

A pilot plant for isotope separation. Established in 2002, laser enrichment experiments were carried out there, however, the plant has been shut down since Iran declared it has no intentions of enriching uranium using the laser isotope separation technique.

Lavizan

All buildings at the former Lavizan-Shian Technical Research Center site were demolished between August 2003 and March 2004 and topsoil has been removed. Environmental samples taken by IAEA inspectors show no trace of radiation. The site is to be returned to the City of Teheran.

Natanz

A hardened Fuel Enrichment Plant (FEP) covering 100,000 square metres that is built 8 meters underground and protected by a concrete wall 2.5 meters thick, itself protected by another concrete wall. In 2004 the roof was hardened with reinforced concrete and covered with 22 metres of earth. The complex consists of two 25,000 square meter halls and a number of administrative buildings. This once secret site was one of the two exposed by Alireza Jafarzadeh in 2002. IAEA Director General Mohamed ElBaradei visited the site on 21 February 2003 and reported that 160 centrifuges were complete and ready for operation, with 1000 more under construction at the site.

Parchin

The Parchin Military Complex is not a nuclear site. This was confirmed on 1 November 2005, when the IAEA was given access to the site and environmental samples were taken. Inspectors did not observe any unusual activities in the buildings visited, and the results of the analysis of environmental samples did not indicate the presence of nuclear material.

Saghand

Location of Irans first uranium ore mines, expected to become operational by March 2005. The deposit is estimated to contain 3,000 to 5,000 tons of uranium oxide at a density of about 500 ppm over an area of 100 to 150 square kilometers.

Tehran

The Tehran Nuclear Research Center (TNRC) is managed by the Atomic Energy Organization of Iran (AEOI). It is equipped with a U.S.-supplied 5-megawatt nuclear research reactor capable of producing 600g of plutonium annually in spent fuel. 17 years production would be sufficient to make a single atomic bomb, however storage of the waste is closely monitored by the IAEA and extracting the plutonium is not possible while Iran maintains its status as a signatory to the nuclear non-proliferation treaty.

Yazd

Radiation processing center.

Economic War

Some say Iran does not pose a threat to the United State because of its nuclear projects,

its WMD, or its support to terrorists organizations as the American administration is claiming, but in its attempt to re-shape the global economical system by converting it from a petrodollar to a petroeuro system. Such conversion is looked upon as a flagrant declaration of economical war against the US that would devastate the revenues of the American corporations and eventually might cause an economic collapse.

In June of 2004 Iran declared its intention of setting up an international oil exchange (a bourse denominated in the Euro currency. Many oil-producing as well as oil-consuming countries had expressed their welcome to such petroeuro bourse. The Iranian reports had stated that this bourse may start its trade with the beginning of 2006. Naturally such an oil bourse would compete against Londons International Petroleum Exchange (IPE), as well as against the New York Mercantile Exchange (NYMEX), both owned by American corporations.

Oil consuming countries have no choice but use the American Dollar to purchase their oil, since the Dollar has been so far the global standard monetary fund for oil exchange. This necessitates these countries to keep the Dollar in their central banks as their reserve fund, thus strengthening the American economy. But if Iran followed by the other oil-producing countries offered to accept the

Euro as another choice for oil exchange the American economy would suffer a real disaster. We could witness this crisis at the end of 2005 and beginning of 2006 when oil investors would have the choice to pay $57 a barrel of oil at the American (NYMEX) and at Londons (IPE), or pay 37 Euros a barrel at the Iranian oil bourse. Such choice would reduce trade volumes at both the Dollar-dependent (NYMEX) and the (IPE).

Many countries had studied the conversion from the ever weakening petrodollar to the gradually strengthening petroeuro system. The de-valuation of the Dollar was caused by the American economy shying away from manufacturing local products — except those of the military -, by outsourcing the American jobs to the cheaper third world countries and depending only on the general service sector, and by the huge cost of two major wars that are still going on. Foreign investors started withdrawing their money from the shaky American market causing further devaluation of the Dollar.

The keen observer of the money market could have noticed that the devaluation of the American Dollar had started since November 2002, while the purchasing power of European Euro had crept upward to reach nowadays to $1.34. Compared to the Japanese Yen the Dollar had dropped from 104.45 to 103.90 yen. The British pound climbed another notch from $1.9122 to $1.9272.

Economic reports published at the beginning of this month (March) had pointed towards the deep dive of the American economy and to the quick rise of the deficit up to $665.90 billion at the end of 2004. The worst is still to come. These numbers worried the international banks, who had sent some warnings to the Bush administration.

In its economical war Iran is treading the same path Saddam Hussein had started when he, in 2000, converted all his reserve from the Dollar to the Euro, and demanded payments in Euro for Iraqi oil. Many economists then mocked Saddam because he had lost a lot of money in this conversion. Yet they were very surprised when he recuperated his losses within less than a year period due to the valuation of the Euro. The American administration became aware of the threat when central banks of many countries started keeping Euros along side of Dollars as their monetary reserve and as an exchange fund for oil (Russian and Chinese central banks in 2003).

There is only one technical obstacle concerning the use of a euro-based oil exchange system, which is the lack of a euro-denominated oil pricing standard, or oil marker as it is referred to in the industry. The three current oil markers are U.S. dollar denominated, which include the West Texas Intermediate crude (WTI), Norway Brent crude, and the UAE Dubai crude. Yet this did not stop Iran from requiring payments in the euro currency for its European and Asian oil exports since spring 2003.

Irans determination in using the petroeuro is inviting in other countries such as Russia and Latin American countries, and even some Saudi investors especially after the Saudi/American relations have weakened lately.

The question now is what should the American administration do? Should we invade Iran as it did Iraq? The American troops are knee-deep in the Iraqi swamp. The global community except for Britain and Italy is not offering any military relief to the US. Thus an American strike against Iran is very unlikely. Iran is not Iraq; it has a more robust military power. Iran has anti-ship missiles based in Abu Mousa island that controls the strait of Hermuz at the entrance of the Persian Gulf. Iran could easily close the strait thus blocking all naval traffic carrying gulf oil to the rest of the world causing a global oil crisis.

The price of an oil barrel could reach up to $120. The US could not achieve regime change by spreading chaos the same way we did to Mussadaqs regime in 1953 since Iranians are aware of such a tactic. Iranians have a patriotic pride of what they call their bomb.

Leaked reports had revealed that Israeli forces are training for such an attack expected to take place June 2007. Israelis have a valid concern regarding and Iranian bomb. Such an bomb would threaten Israels security. Further more the bomb would force the US to enter into negotiations.

Iran had invested a lot of money and effort to obtain nuclear technology and would never abandon it as evident in its political rhetoric. Unlike Iraq Iran would not keep quiet of Israel strikes its nuclear facilities. Iran would retaliate aggressively which may lead to the destabilization of the whole region including Israel, Gulf States, Iraq, and even Afghanistan. It is evident from Irans behavior that it isnt playing around and that it means business. A preemptive strike on Iran is justified at this point, I strongly urge the policy makers to consider an air strike on Irans nuclear sites within the next year or so.

The Mullahs are determined to control the region and would stop at nothing to gain total domination.

Irans Neighbors

Irans relations with the Gulf Arab countries operate on two tracks. On the one hand, Iran has a decided need to cultivate friends, escape regional isolation, and continue important trade relations. On the other hand, it nurtures a desire to assert an independent and forceful foreign policy. In view of recent Iranian behavior towards the GCC countries, one can question whether Irans leaders have the skill and acumen to balance these two often contradictory goals. Indeed, relations between Iran and its Arab neighbors have been strained for decades especially since the revolution. Fearful of Shia revivalism, most Arab states supported Iraq during the Iran-Iraq War and paid huge sums of money to sustain Saddam Husseins war effort. The shock and trauma of Iraqs invasion of Kuwait in 1990 put all the GCC countries on notice that they could quite literally be invaded by aggressive neighbors. Given the vast asymmetries in population and wealth between the GCC and countries such as Iran, Iraq, and Yemen, it is not surprising that security is of paramount concern.

Even though the US umbrella provides a strong deterrent against major aggression of the kind that occurred in 1990, the American presence may be less effective against political threats and subversion. Given the complicated sociology of most GCC countries large foreign populations and the diverse ethnic and religious backgrounds of all residents internal security issues are an increasingly important factor in regional stability. In this context, the Iranian threat looms large.

The Gulf states seem to have grown increasingly apprehensive that Iran is determined to become the regional hegemon. Moreover, whatever conciliatory action Iran may have been willing to take have been obscured by its aggressive tactics over control and sovereignty of Abu Musa Island and Tunb Islands. Irans claim to the islands has generated widespread apprehension. What began as a dispute between Sharja and Iran escalated to a dispute with the United Arab Emirates (UAE), then the GCC, and then to the Arab League. The issue is one of principle, but strong strategic overtones also exist. If Iran were to gain sovereignty over the islands, it could extend its territorial waters into large areas that contain much oil. The UAE has proposed submitting the dispute to the International Court of Justice for resolution. To date, however, Iran has refused to accept this course of reconciliation. So long as the dispute remains unresolved and Iran continues to occupy and reinforce Abu Musa, tensions between Iran and the GCC will continue and could escalate.

Since the Iraqi invasion of Kuwait in August 1990, Kuwait, Bahrain, Qatar, and Oman have all signed defense-cooperation agreements with the United States; the UAE also signed an agreement on 25 July 1994. A less formalized arrangement with Saudi Arabia is also in place.

A similar kinds of actions were involved in the various military agreements. The agreement with Bahrain expanded a previous agreement to include a joint exercise program, access to ports and airfields, and prepositioning of some equipment. The US and Kuwait signed a 10-year agreement allowing the US access to ports and facilities, prepositioning of military equipment and joint military training. American officials renewed an existing facilities-access agreement with Oman. As a result of Saddams moves in October 1994, Kuwait agreed to base a squadron of US planes and to expand the number of US tanks stored in the kingdom. Qatar agreed to store a brigades worth of armor. Since the end of the Gulf War, allied aircraft have been based in Saudi Arabia to enforce the no-fly zone.

Over the next 10 years, Iran will pose serious challenges to its neighbors, and its actions will continue to need deterring. Thus, an American military presence will remain necessary to the security of the region. Yet, Iran also feels threatened, and its own insecurities may contribute to the dynamics of threat escalation. The leadership in Tehran presently feels beleaguered, paranoid, and intimidated by changes occurring both in the neighborhood and in the international environment.

Irans mullahs are fighting a rear-guard action to save a revolution, and the removal of one or two leaders will make little difference to the governance of the country. Without a doubt, the unpopularity of the Iranian regime is second only to the impotence of the opposition, both inside and outside the country. Most Iranians would support the removal of the clerics from power. Irans rejection of the Arab-Israeli peace process and its support for regimes and groups intent on using force to overthrow legitimate governments ensure continued conflict with moderate states in the Middle East and outside powers, especially the United States. Indeed, Irans leaders have rejected American calls for an official dialogue to discuss major points of contention. Although significant voices in Tehran have wanted such a dialogue in the past, the fundamentalist headed by Khamenei have effectively shot down any prospects for talks in the near future. Many American observers of Iranian politics believe that the radicals fear American military power less than the prospect of Americas establishing itself as the leader of Western secularism and the generator of a global culture that threatens the very essence of the revolution. Irans ability to influence political events in the Middle East is clearly linked to other factors over which it has only marginal if any control. A revolution in Algeria leading to the establishment of an Islamic regime could have profound implications for the stability of the Mediterranean, including Egypt. A collapse of the Arab-Israeli peace process, aided and abetted by Iranian interference, also could have a profound and negative domino effect on the region. The resurgence of Saddam Hussein or an equally ruthless successor in Iraq could likewise spell danger.

From an American perspective, the search for an optimum policy towards Iran and the Gulf remains illusive and fraught with dangers. At one level, military cooperation with the GCC has gone from strength to strength, and the deployments of American forces to Kuwait during October 1994 demonstrated that it will be a long time before either Iran or Iraq can directly challenge the US and GCC with military force. However, the political and sociological dimensions of Gulf security pose more complicated problems. Without GCC cooperation, the US will not be able to protect the Gulf from major threats. The stability of the Gulf will depend on how well the US can maintain a delicate balance between security needs and political action.

Oil Weapon

The officials of the Islamic Republic of Iran have threatened that if the United Nations Organization adopts serious sanctions against the regime of Iran (due to the nuclear case of Iran which is currently in the Security Council of the UNO), they may resort to the oil weapon. This threat has been also used in the past for countering the Western efforts for stopping the Iranian nuclear program of Iran and the struggle to get the regime in Iran changed from the Islamic Republic to something else. But, what is the oil weapon and what does it mean for the regime of Iran and the others?

It seems that the oil weapon is anything that could be used to stop or hinder the flow of the much-needed oil to the international markets. This could include a wide range of actions that intentionally stop or seriously reduce the flow of oil from the oil exporting countries to the main consumption centers.

The expression of oil weapon has been used in the past by various sources to refer to different notions. Some people have indicated to the possible use of the Iran oil Bourse which may use Euro for oil transactions, as one of the sources of the oil weapon. It has also been widely used in the media to refer to the case of the oil embargo in the 1973 style (that Arab oil producing countries tried to use the oil leverage against the West due to supporting the Israel in the war with its Arab neighbors). Also, The terrorists that wish to make troubles for the internal and external enemies of the concerned persons or organizations have also used it as a means for their aims. However, what the Iranian authorities have been referring to is not a general oil embargo or a group action, or a terrorist act.

Although some Iranian officials have invited the Muslim oil exporting countries in the past to consider a group action in the field of oil supplies in order to exert pressure on the Western states (to reduce or stop supporting the Zionists or Israel), it is almost certain that in the present case of Irans quarrel with the Western states (especially the USA), no other country is going to join Iranian regime in the usage of oil weapon and turn this move into a general action. Terrorist actions may be included in the plans of Iran to use oil weapon but they will be only a part of the last resorts and the Iranian Kamikaze.

Any action by Iran to stop the oil flow from the Persian Gulf countries, by blocking the strait Hurmoz, attacking the shipping lines, trying to blow up the pipelines or the production and refinery facilities of the other countries in the region (such as Azerbaijan, Kazakhstan, and Turkmenistan in the Caspian Sea, or Saudi Arabia, Kuwait, Iraq, Qatar, the United Arab Emirates, Oman, Bahrain in the Persian Gulf), will be considered as a serious violation of the international laws and regulations for the concerned states. It would be in practice like giving a declaration of war to them. At the same time, it would be a serious challenge to the interests of the major oil importing states, especially the USA, that according to the Carter Doctrine considers the Persian Gulf as an area of vital interests. The US government feels obliged to stop any serious challenge to its vital interest, by all means, including the military actions.

In fact, once in the past the struggle of the Iranian regime during the Iran-Iraq war (1980-88) lead to a serious confrontation of Iran with the US forces in the region. According to the Wilipedia on 18 April 1988, the US Navy waged a one day battle against Iranian forces in and around the [Hormuz] strait. The battle, dubbed Operation Praying Mantis by the US side, was launched in retaliation for the 14 April mining of the USS Samuel B. Roberts (FFG-58). US forces sank two Iranian warships and as many as six armed speedboats in the engagement, which was the largest between surface forces since the World War II.

Can Iran block the Hormuz Strait?

The Strait of Hormuz is the narrow sea passage that connects the Persian Gulf to the Oman Sea. This is the only sea-passage for the export of oil from the Persian Gulf states. The Iranian forces have done several maneuvers aimed at closing the Strait of Hormuz at the time of crisis and the Western forces in the region (in cooperation with the some of the littoral countries or independently) have conducted several maneuvers aimed at deterring such plans. Peter Brooks, a senior fellow at the Heritage Foundation, writes: Iran could temporarily wreak havoc in the Persian Gulf, using sea-skimming, nears supersonic Chinese C-801 anti-ship cruise missiles (and older Silkworm missiles), quiet Russian Kilo diesel and mini-submarines, stealthy mines, high speed patrol boats swarm tactics.

Iran plans to begin offensive operations by launching successive waves of explosives-packed boats against U.S. warships in the Gulf, piloted by Ashura or suicide bombers. The first wave can draw on more than 1,000 small fast-attack boats operated by the Revolutionary Guards navy, equipped with rocket launchers, heavy machine-guns and possibly Sagger anti-tank missiles?A second wave of suicide attacks would be carried out by suicide submarines and semi-submersible boats, before Iran deploys its Russian-built Kilo-class submarines and Chinese-built Huodong missile boats to attack U.S. warships, the source said. The 114-foot Chinese boats are equipped with advanced radar-guided C-802s, a sea-skimming cruise missile with a 60-mile range against which many U.S. naval analysts believe there is no effective defense...The Iranians also plan to lay huge minefields across the Persian Gulf inside the Strait of Hormuz, effectively trapping ships that manage to cross the Strait before they can enter the Gulf, where they can be destroyed by coastal artillery and land-based Silkworm missile batteries. Today, Iran has sophisticated EM-53 bottom-tethered mines, which it purchased from China in the 1990s. The EM-53 presents a serious threat to major U.S. surface vessels, since its rocket-propelled charge is capable of hitting the hull of its target at speeds in excess of 70 miles per hour. Some analysts believe it can knock out a U.S. aircraft carrier. More recently, the semi-official Iranian news agency has reported: ...Iran successfully test-fired a super-modern flying boat on Tuesday during war games at the Strait of Hormuz, the Mehr News Agency correspondent in the region reported. The boat is capable of moving at high speeds of up to 100 knots in the Persian Gulf waters and the Oman Sea. Because of its advanced design, no radar at sea or in the air can locate it. It can lift out of the water and can launch missiles with precise targeting while moving. A new land-to-sea missile called Kowsar was also tested successfully.

Therefore, it seems that Iran has actually enough power to block the Strait of Hormuz by sinking several big ships in the main channels of the traffic (although most of the traffic separation lines are in the side of the Strait which are technically, i.e. according to the international law of Seas, part of Omans Territorial waters. Also, Iran may interrupt the shipping in the Strait of Hormuz by mining the international waterway or directly attacking the target vessels. Such actions are enough to stat a full-scale war between the regime of Iran and all other concerned force.

However, at the present time, what Iranian regime is referring to as the oil weapon is only stopping the flow of Iranian oil to the market. Iran produces about 4 million barrels a day and exports 2.4 million barrels a day. The oil market is volatile at moment due to several reasons. Cutting the oil input of Iran from the international markets would certainly lead to a serious increase of the prices. It may reach the level of 100-120 dollars per barrel.

This is going to be two-sided weapon. The oil prices over a hundred dollar will have serious consequences for the international economy. However, Iran as an oil exporting country will be in a difficult situation if the export of oil is stopped. Irans government derives about 50% of its revenues and most of its foreign currency from oil sales Iran is not only relying on the oil revenues for its economy, but also it is an importer of the oil products. Iran has not the capacity to produce enough gasoline for the internal consumption and it has to import a major part of its needs from other countries. (In recent years, Oman has been a major source of gasoline imports for Iran). According to Peter Kiernan: ...although Iran is the second largest producer in OPEC, its domestic refining capacity does not meet local demand, and it must import about 170,000 bpd of gasoline, which costs it as much as $4 billion a year... Also, Ilan Berman writes a closer look indicates that the oil weapon, whether in the form of reductions in Iranian output or military moves in the Hormuz Strait, is likely to be a double-edged sword for the Islamic Republic...in their planning, the Bush Administration and its international partners would do well to take doomsday predictions about Iranian energy leverage with a grain of salt. But they should also be thinking carefully about the economic and political costs of inaction. Simply put, Washington must ask itself whether the world would be better off with a temporary spike in energy prices created by a serious Iran strategy, or with a permanent hike in the cost of doing business in a region dominated by an atomic Islamic Republic.

Eventually the countries that have problems with the regime of Iran (for its policies in the Middle East peace process, supporting terrorism, trying to expand Islamic revolution, and of course the nuclear program of Iran) have to decide that a 100 dollar (per barrel) oil is more dangerous or survival of a regime like the one that is in power in Iran and it may get its hand on the nuclear weapons.

Condoleezza Rice, the US Secretary of State, has played down the threat of Iran for using the oil weapon. For instance, following the threats from the Ayatollah Ali Khamenei, the Supreme Leader of Iran, she said: We should not place too much emphasis on a threat of this kind.

It seems that the concerned countries in the region are not going to tare the threats of Iran so lightly. Some of the actions that are gradually taking place in response to such threats are:

1-   Trying to reduce the reliance to the Persian Gulf oil, through finding alternative sources, such as the Caspian Sea region.

2-   Reducing reliance of the oil exporting countries of the Persian Gulf on the Persian Gulf (especially the Strait of Hormuz) and persuading the exports from the Red Sea (although it makes the supply far from some of the most important centers of demand such as China and India).

3-   Trying to restore the Iraqi oil supplies as a replacement for the possible cutting of the Iranian oil.

4-   Using the floating super tankers that keep the oil in the regions out of the Persian Gulf and ready to be traded.

5-   Expanding the oil storage facilities in the major consumption centers. There is also news of storage facilities of the Saudi Arabia in China. Paul Rogers has written in the Energy Bulletin ...A refinery for Saudi oil is already being built in Fujian, and a joint refinery venture is planned for Qingdao. Perhaps more significant is the plan to build a strategic oil-reserve facility in a coastal location in southeast China, the aim being to supply and store Saudi oil in which can be used in times of conflict and disruption of supplies.

6-   Expansion of the pipelines in the region. These pipelines take the oil and gas from the Persian Gulf region to the places like the Mediterranean and Red Sea.

Ayatollah Ali Khamenei, Irans Supreme Leader, has given a warning that Iran would disrupt the oil shipments in the Persian Gulf if the USA makes a wrong move in the confrontation with Iran over the nuclear program of Iran.

As such, the evidence in Iraq indicates that disruption in the flow of oil is one of the main objects of the terrorist organizations in that country. Also, the Al-qaeda and its main operatives have many times asked for and tried to use the disruption in the oil flow through terrorist actions. The aims of terrorists in this field are: 1- they create problems for the destination countries, especially the West, 2- Cut or slow down the income of the exporting countries, and 3- put pressure on the people of the target countries through reduction of the availability of the oil and its products.

Irans Revolutionary Guards are making preparations for a massive assault on U.S. naval forces and international shipping in the Persian Gulf, according to a former Iranian intelligence officer who defected to the West in 2001.

The plans, which include the use of bottom-tethered mines potentially capable of destroying U.S. aircraft carriers, were designed to counter a U.S. land invasion and to close the Strait of Hormuz, the defector said in a phone interview from his home in Europe.

They would also be triggered if the United States or Israel launched a pre-emptive strike on Iran to knock out nuclear and missile facilities.

Between 15 and 16.5 million barrels of oil transit the Strait of Hormuz each day, roughly 20 percent of the worlds daily oil production, according to the U.S.

governments Energy Information Administration.

The overall plans are being coordinated by the intelligence office of the Ministry of Defense, known as HFADA.

Revolutionary Guards missile units have identified more than 100 targets, including Saudi oil production and oil export centers, the defector said. They have more than 45 to 50 Shahab-3 and Shahab-4 missiles ready for shooting against those targets and against Israel, he added.

A U.S. military intelligence official, while unable to authenticate the documents without seeing them, recognized the Strategic Studies Center and noted that the individual whose name appears as the author of the plan, Abbas Motaj, was head of the Iranian navy until late 2005.

A former Revolutionary Guards officer, contacted by NewsMax in Europe, immediately recognized the Naval Strategic Studies institute from its Persian-language acronym, NDAJA. He provided independent information on recent deployments of Shahab-3 missiles that coincided with information contained in the NDAJA plan.

The Iranian contingency plan is summarized in an Order of Battle map, which schematically lays out Irans military and strategic assets and how they will be used against U.S. military forces from the Strait of Hormuz up to Busheir.

The map identifies three major areas of operations, called mass kill zones, where Iranian strategists believe they can decimate a U.S.-led invasion force before it actually enters the Persian Gulf.

The kill zones run from the low-lying coast just to the east of Bandar Abbas, Irans main port that sits in the bottleneck of the Strait of Hormuz, to the ports of Jask and Shah Bahar on the Indian Ocean, beyond the Strait.

Behind the kill zones are strategic missile launchers labeled as area of chemical operations, area of biological warfare operations, and area where nuclear operations start.

Irans overall battle management will be handled through C4I and surveillance satellites. It is unclear in the documents shared with NewsMax whether this refers to commercial satellites or satellite intelligence obtained from allies, such as Russia or China. Iran has satellite cooperation programs with both nations.

The map is labeled the current status of military forces in the Persian Gulf and the Strait of Hormuz, 1384. 1384 is the Iranian year that ends on March 20, 2006.

ran plans to begin offensive operations by launching successive waves of explosives-packed boats against U.S. warships in the Gulf, piloted by Ashura or suicide bombers. The first wave can draw on more than 1,000 small fast-attack boats operated by the Revolutionary Guards navy, equipped with rocket launchers, heavy machine-guns and possibly Sagger anti-tank missiles.

In recent years, the Iranians have used these small boats to practice swarming raids on commercial vessels and U.S. warships patrolling the Persian Gulf.

The White House listed two such attacks in the list of 10 foiled al-Qaida terrorist attacks it released on Feb. 10. The attacks were identified as a plot by al-Qaida operatives to attack ships in the [Persian] Gulf in early 2003, and a separate plot to attack ships in the Strait of Hormuz.

A second wave of suicide attacks would be carried out by suicide submarines and semi-submersible boats, before Iran deploys its Russian-built Kilo-class submarines and Chinese-built Huodong missile boats to attack U.S. warships, the source said.

Admiral Redd was appointed to head the National Counterterrorism Center last year.

Irans naval strategists believe the U.S. will attempt to

land ground forces to the east of Bandar Abbas. Their plans call for extensive use of ground-launched tactical missiles, coastal artillery, as swell as strategic missiles aimed at Saudi Arabia and Israel tipped with chemical, biological and possibly nuclear warheads.

The Iranians also plan to lay huge minefields across the Persian Gulf inside the Strait of Hormuz, effectively trapping ships that manage to cross the Strait before they can enter the Gulf, where they can be destroyed by coastal artillery and land-based Silkworm missile batteries.

Today, Iran has sophisticated EM-53 bottom-tethered mines, which it purchased from China in the 1990s. The EM-53 presents a serious threat to major U.S. surface vessels, since its rocket-propelled charge is capable of hitting the hull of its target at speeds in excess of 70 miles per hour. Some analysts believe it can knock out a U.S. aircraft carrier.

The Joint Chiefs of Staff has been warning about Irans growing naval buildup in the Persian Gulf for over a decade, and in a draft presidential finding submitted to President Clinton in late February 1995, concluded that Iran already had the capability to close the Strait of Hormuz.

Chapter 8
Ruling Mullahs, Al-Qaeda And Hezbollah

U.S. intelligence agencies are investigating whether senior al-Qaida leaders hiding in Iran may have helped to plan or coordinate the terrorist bombings that killed 34 people, including eight Americans, late Monday in Saudi Arabia. Intelligence officials said several al-Qaida leaders, including Saif al Adel, whos wanted in connection with the 1998 bombings of two U.S. embassies in Africa and may now be the terrorist groups third-ranking official, and Osama bin Ladens son Saad have found refuge in Iran, where they remain active.

National Security Adviser Condoleezza Rice, speaking to foreign journalists in Washington on Wednesday, made no mention of a possible link between al-Qaida members in Iran and the Saudi bombings but said: We are concerned about al-Qaida operating in Iran.

The Iranian government has expelled more than 500 lower-ranking al-Qaida members and denies harboring any of the groups senior leaders. But the U.S. officials, who all spoke on the condition of anonymity, said there was evidence that members of Irans Revolutionary Guard were sheltering al Adel, the younger bin Laden, other al-Qaida leaders and some other members of bin Ladens family. The officials emphasized that no hard evidence has been found that al-Qaida fugitives in Iran had a hand in the Saudi bombings.

If the CIA or other intelligence agencies find evidence confirming suspicions that the Saudi bombings were planned or supported from Iran, one senior U.S. official warned Wednesday, the conversation with Iran could become a confrontation. Asked what the administrations options would be in that case, another senior official conceded that trying to seize al Adel and others would be extremely difficult, but added: The military option is never off the table.

The suspicions of a link between Iran and the bombings are focused largely on al Adel, who some U.S. officials think is now the head of al-Qaida operations in the Persian Gulf.

While it found no operational ties between al Qaeda and Iraq, the 911 commission investigating the attacks has concluded that Osama bin Ladens Al-Qaeda network had long running dealings with Iraqs neighbor and historic foe, Iran.

Al Qaeda, may even have played a yet unknown role in helping Hezbollah militants in the 1996 bombing of the Khobar Towers complex in Saudi Arabia, an attack the United States has long blamed solely on Hezbollah and its Iranian sponsors.

The idea that bin Laden may have had a hand in the Khobar bombing would mark a rare operational alliance between Sunni and Shiite Muslim groups that have historically been at odds.

In relation to Iran, 911 commission investigators said

intelligence showed far greater potential for collaboration between Hezbollah and al Qaeda than many had previously thought. Iran is a primary sponsor of Hezbollah, or Party of God, the Lebanon-based anti-Israel group that has been designated a terrorist organization by the United States. The commissions Republican chairman, former New Jersey governor Thomas H. Kean, also said in a television appearance that there were a lot more active contacts, frankly, with Iran and with Pakistan than there were with Iraq.

But perhaps most startling was the commissions finding that bin Laden may have played a role in the Khobar attack. Although previous court filings and testimony indicated that al Qaeda and Iranian elements had contacts during the 1990s, U.S. authorities have not publicly linked bin Laden or his operatives to that strike, which killed 19 U.S. servicemen.

Bruce Hoffman, a terrorism expert who heads the Washington office of Rand Corp., said that although bin Ladens then-fledgling group was an early suspect in the blasts, the evidence kept pointing to an Iranian connection, so people tended to discount a bin Laden connection.

The broader notion of links between bin Ladens group and Hezbollah or hard-line elements in Irans security forces has been a hot topic in U.S. law enforcement and intelligence circles for years. Many analysts have viewed such an alliance as dubious, largely because of ancient animosities between Shiite and Sunni Muslims. Several leaders of al Qaeda, a Sunni organization, have issued rabidly anti-Shiite proclamations.

United States previously compiled evidence of limited contacts between Iranian interests and al Qaeda. U.S. officials alleged that Iran was harboring al Qaeda militants who had fled neighboring Afghanistan after the U.S. invasion there.

Iran has denied that al Qaeda was operating from its territory, and announced earlier this year that it would put on trial a dozen suspected members of the terrorist group. The original U.S. indictment of bin Laden, filed in 1998, said al Qaeda forged alliances with the government of Iran and its associated terrorist group Hezbollah for the purpose of working together against their perceived common enemies in the West, particularly the United States.

There were reports in the months preceding the attack that bin Laden was seeking to facilitate a shipment of explosives to Saudi Arabia. On the day of the attack, bin Laden was congratulated by al Qaeda militants, the report says.

The report recounts some of the previously alleged contacts between al Qaeda and Iran or Hezbollah and concludes, We have seen strong but indirect evidence that bin Ladens organization did in fact play some as yet unknown role in the Khobar attack.

The report also says that several years before the Khobar attack, bin Ladens representatives and Iranian officials had discussed putting aside Shia-Sunni divisions to cooperate against the common enemy. A group of al Qaeda representatives then traveled to Iran and to Hezbollah training camps in Lebanon for training in explosives, intelligence and security, the report says.

Bin Laden himself, the report added, showed particular interest in Hezbollahs truck bombing tactics in Lebanon in 1983 that killed 241 U.S. Marines.

Flynt L. Leverett, a Middle East expert in the Clinton and Bush administrations who is now a Brookings Institution scholar, said active cooperation between al Qaeda and Iran cannot be ruled out as wholly implausible.

There are going to be serious structural limits to how

much al Qaeda and Iran might cooperate, Leverett said. Within those limits, though, there is some room for very tactical and self-serving cooperation between al Qaeda and some parts of Iranian intelligence. Leverett cited as an example the allegations that Iran had harbored al Qaeda operatives fleeing Afghanistan.

The Tehran government is holding several top-level Al Qaeda operatives that, experts say, could lead to the biggest breakthrough in curtailing the organization since the fall of Afghanistan.Though the Iranians havent mentioned any names, intelligence officials and press reports indicate theyve captured Saad bin Laden, Osama bin Ladens son, who has assumed a leadership role; Sulaiman Abu Ghaith, the Al Qaeda spokesman; and Saif al-Adel, the latest No. 3 who is believed to be in charge of military operations.

Even more significant, according to one Western intelligence official, Tehran is also holding Al Qaedas No. 2, Ayman al-Zawahiri, who is known as an Islamic fundamentalist intellectual and eloquent speaker for the organization. While some US intelligence sources have expressed doubt that Iran really has Dr. Zawahiri, the European official says Tehran absolutely has him.

If so, his capture, along with that of the other top members, would deal a major blow to the terrorist network. Zawahiri would be an incredible blow, says Stanley Bedlington, a former senior analyst in the CIAs counterterrorism center. All four of them would be a tremendous blow.... Al Qaeda will continue to rebuild, but it will take a lot of time to get new leadership with those sorts of skills and experience.

Whether Iran will hand them over is another question. The senior Western intelligence official says a European country is involved in negotiating some kind of turnover now. It would be difficult for Iran to directly turn them over to the US for the obvious political considerations: It is an Islamic country named as both a sponsor of terrorism and a member of the axis of evil by the US.

Moreover, the US accuses Tehran of trying to develop nuclear weapons and is pressuring it to stop. Conversely, Iran would like the US to stop supporting Mujahideen e-Khalq, a group that opposes the Iranian regime and operates freely in the US.

I suspect that some Iranians would argue that keeping some of these high-ranking Al Qaeda members incarcerated is a good bargaining chip, says Ali Ansari, a Middle East historian at Durham University in England.

Publicly, both sides are being predictably circumspect at the moment. Iran has only said it is holding a large number of small- and big-time Al Qaeda members.

In response, the US has sounded unimpressed, perhaps as means of applying additional pressure. We have said all along we believe that there were senior members of Al Qaeda that were operating from Iran, State Department spokesman Richard Boucher said last week. He noted that the US has made clear that the Iranians - if they are in fact holding the captives rather than harboring them - should deport them to where theyre wanted for crimes, or to their home countries.

Whos who of Al Qaeda in Iran

Al Qaeda leaders supposedly being held in Iran include some of the most prominent and well-educated among the group. Zawahiri has been Mr. bin Ladens No. 2 for several years, his personal physician, and closest intellectual sparring partner. He has written several books on fundamental Islam as well as communications for Al Qaeda.

Zawahiri was raised and educated in Cairo, where he became a doctor and a member, and eventually a leader, of the Egyptian Islamic Jihad (EIJ). He left Egypt in the early 1980s, after serving a three-year sentence for a part in the assassination of Egypts President Anwar Sadat. He then made his way to Afghanistan, where he dedicated his medical services to the Afghan mujahideen fighting the former Soviet Union. He later united his wing of EIJ with Al Qaeda.

Zawahiri is a very important thinker and writer, the intelligence official says. His pen is going to be missed.

Mr. Adel, also known as Mohammed Makkawi, is also a former member of EIJ, and he served as a colonel in the Egyptian Armys special forces. Adel is believed to have trained and fought the tribal fighters who ambushed and killed the 18 US Army Rangers in Mogadishu in 1993. He helped plan the 1998 attacks on the US Embassies in Africa, and he was a key planner of the 2000 attack on the USS Cole. Moreover, he is believed to be part of a tactical alliance between Al Qaeda and Hizbullah.

Saad bin Laden is one of Osama bin Ladens oldest sons, believed to be in his early 30s and a rising star in Al Qaeda. Officials say he has provided financial and logistical support for several operations, including the April 11, 2002, bombing of a synagogue in Tunisia that killed 19 people.

Sulaiman Abu Ghaith is a Kuwaiti, who was a teacher of Islamic studies, an imam, and a member of the Muslim Brotherhood. Kuwait eventually suspended him from religious activities for criticizing the government. He spent two months in Bosnia in 1994, where he fought with Muslim forces. He then returned to Kuwait. After the start of US strikes on Afghanistan in 2001, Abu Ghaith appeared on Al Jazeera as an Al Qaeda spokesman.

Below is Top Secret Memo From the Office of **Ali Akbar Nateqeh-Nouri,** the director of Supreme Leaders Intelligence Service Operational Unit 43 (English translation of original document turn in by undercover reporter.

Re: Instructions to increase the level of support and cooperation between Al-Qaeda and Hezbollah.

**Supreme Leader Intelligence Head Quarters –
Extremely Confidential
To: Head of the Operative Unit 43
Re: Direct Orders from the Supreme Leader
Hojat ol Islam Mr. Pour-Ghanad:
With regards & prayers,**

The success and achievements of your dedicated and brave team is our wish. Your report on different strategies in support of future Al-Qaida plans has been reviewed from a variety of different perspectives. In clarifying any doubts, his Excellency Supreme Leader has insisted on reminding us all that, combating with the International Imperialism, at the head of which, America & Israel are the main two enemies of Islamic order, is the main goal of our Islamic Directive. Disruption and destruction of their economic and political systems, discrediting, and endangering all of their other structural organizations and balance of security of these two united enemies of Islamic regime are crucial and an obligatory task to be achieved. His Excellency has asked for *more attentiveness on these activities, with emphasis on your outmost awareness and alertness. With due consideration of the downfalls and consequences of this cooperation, persist in organized groups, and in closer collaboration with other intelligence and security operatives and outside supporters, to limit our enemies increasing array of activities. Reflecting all your achievements under the direct supervision of the head of the department of Hefazat, - - (Special Intelligence Operatives within organizations) - - detection of any failure will be naturally the task of this dedicated office. Also it has been assigned for our future conferences to further rectify and discuss the elimination of major obstacles, additional implementation of improvements **with regards to achieving a higher level of cooperation between Al-Qaida fighters and Hezbollah fighters towards a specific ideal goal.** At the end, his Excellency Supreme Leader with satisfaction and complete support for the achievement of your future plans and understanding the importance of your duties, his Excellency Supreme Leader has also insisted - - **you must make sure, that no trace of any support for Al-Qaida, which could have negative and irreversible consequences should ever exist and be limited to the current relationship with Moghnie and Al Zarghavi.** - -*

**God be with you,
Ali Akbar Nategh Nouri
Head of Supreme Leader Intelligence Office
Extremely Confidential**

Note: The signatory of this document is none other than the notorious Mullah, Nateqeh-Nouri who was Khatamis - - ostensible - - opponent in the 1997 elections.

In the immediate aftermath of 9-11, the conventional

wisdom in the intelligence community was that the Shiite Hezbollah and the Sunni al Qaeda did not and could not operate together because of the religious divide between the two groups.

However, al Qaedas own writings, and testimony of senior al Qaeda operatives in U.S. custody (Jamal al Fadl) recount the extensive contacts bewtween the two organizations while bin Laden was in Sudan, including joint military and explosives training.

It has taken the conventional wisdom a long time to catch up with reality on the ground, but it is important to remember that things that were often considered inconceivable in the shadow infrastructure of non-state actors were simply based on our preconceptions, not reality.

If the Lebanese conflict continued on, it would have been likely that al Qaeda would try to work again with its occassional ally in an alliance of convenience that could benefit both groups. The chaos in the region benefits all the non-state armed groups, and such circumstances often give rise to transitory (or perhaps permanent) alliances between groups that share the same goals and resources. While Zarqawi fanned the flames of the Sunni-Shiite divide inside Iraq, it was in part a tactical decision to weaken the government and cause a civil war, rather than a theological decison.

The point of contact with bin Laden in Sudan was Imad Mugniya, the person currently considered to be Hezbollahs chief of military operations and the likely instigator of the kidnapping of the Israeli soldiers. Mugniya, as noted elsewhere on this blog, has been at this for a long time and the sophisticated operation bear the hallmarks of his style. in addition, his high-level contacts in Iran, and his long-time protection from Irans revolutionary government have given him the ability to operate with impunity and survive for many years.

Since the early 1990s contact between the two groups there have been other interactions. Hezbollah operatives-Aziz Nassour and Samih Osailly- provided the infrastructure for al Qaedas diamond operations in Liberia and Sierra Leone that helped al Qaeda transfer millions of dollars into fungible assets and out of the range of the Wests financial sanctions.

Mugniya has worked extensively in West Africa among the Lebanese diaspora of several hundred thousand that populate the West coast. The Ivory Coast is an especially active place for Hezbollah, both for fund raising and R&R.

The enemy of my enemy is my friend, and in the case of Lebanon, that saying could well apply to Hezbollah and al Qaeda regardless of religious differences.

Chapter 9

Politics and government of Iran

Sharia: (Sharīah) refers to the body of Islamic law. The term means way or path; it is the legal framework within which public and some private aspects of life are regulated for those living in a legal system based on Muslim principles of jurisprudence.

Sharia deals with many aspects of day-to-day life, including politics, economics, banking, business law, contract law, sexuality, and social issues. Some Islamic scholars accept Sharia as the body of precedent and legal theory established before the 19th century, while other scholars view Sharia as a changing body, and include Islamic legal theory from the contemporary period.

Constitution: The Constitution of Islamic Republic of Iran abolished the Constitution of 1906. The 1979 Constitution dates 24 October 1979 and is in force since 3 December 1979[3]. Significant amendments were adopted on 28 July 1989.[4] It is the only constitution in the world to enshrine the principles of mullahcracy.

Supreme Leader of Iran: Guardian Jurisprudent was created in the constitution of the Islamic Republic of Iran as the highest ranking political and religious authority of the nation. The title *Supreme* Leader is often used as a sign of respect, however this terminology does not exist in the constitution.

Ayatollah Ali Khamenei is the current Supreme Leader of Iran.

The Supreme Leader is elected by the Assembly of Experts, which is also in charge of overseeing the Supreme Leader, and has the power to dismiss and replace him at any time. Although the members of the Assembly of Experts are elected by public vote, the Guardian Council (whose fuqaha members are appointed by the Supreme Leader) vets the candidates before the election. Many political analysts believe this creates a **closed loop of power** and many prominent Iranian reformists have voiced their opposition to the current election laws (including Abdollah Noori) but have not been able to bring any changes to the law.

While the Supreme Leader is generally considered as the ultimate head of the Iranian political establishment, the President of Iran, who is elected by direct public vote, is the Executive President (Head of government, directly in charge of the executive branch).

The question of how to fit the Supreme Leader and the President in the theoretical definitions of Head of state and Head of government is as thorny as with the atypical products of various other revolutions, even long after the regimes were constitutionally stabilized, such as the Libyan Guide of the Revolution or the party chairmen in the Soviet model, who systematically outranked both (or may hold one or both posts) politically, or real political power may even clearly with one who (sometimes no longer) holds none such formal positions, as in the Chinese case of Deng Xiaoping for whom the - unofficial- term paramount leader was used; however, *de facto* and *de jure* the Supreme Leaders ideological and political authority is, as the title implies, supreme. While the Supreme Leader lacks crucial attributes of a Head of state (such as the summit position in diplomatic relations; though supreme command is very rarely entrusted to a third office) and of a Head of government (a lead role in daily government) his clear ideological leadership resembles that of a single-party-leader (the Islamic religion holding the guiding prominence instead of a strictly political ideology) and his formalized kingmaker position both that and a paramount leader, be it not behind the curtain.

Functions and duties of The Supreme Leader

- Delineation of the general policies of the Islamic Republic of Iran after consultation with the Nations Expediency Discernment Council.
- Supervision over the proper execution of the general policies of the system.
- Issuing decrees for national referenda.
- Assuming supreme command of the armed forces.
- Declaration of war and peace, and the mobilization of the armed forces.
- Appointment, dismissal, and acceptance of resignation of:
    1. the fuqaha on the Guardian Council.
    2. the supreme judicial authority of the country.

3. the head of the radio and television network of the Islamic Republic of Iran.
4. the chief of the joint staff.
5. the chief commander of the Islamic Revolutionary Guards Corps.
6. the supreme commanders of the armed forces.

- Resolving differences between the three wings of the armed forces and regulation of their relations.
- Resolving the problems, which cannot be solved by conventional methods, through the Nations Exigency Council.
- Signing the decree formalizing the elections in Iran for the President of the republic by the people.
- Dismissal of the President of the Republic, with due regard for the interests of the country, after the Supreme Court holds him guilty of the violation of his constitutional duties, or after a vote of the Islamic Consultative Assembly (The Majlis of Iran) testifying to his incompetence on the basis of Article 89 of the Constitution.
- Pardoning or reducing the sentences of convicts, within the framework of Islamic criteria, on a recommendation (to that effect) from the head of the Judiciary. The Leader may delegate part of his duties and powers to another person.

Incumbents

Since the establishment of the Islamic Republic of Iran, Iran has had two Supreme Leaders: **Ayatollah Ruhollah Khomeini,** 1979–1989.

Acknowledged as the father of the Islamic Revolution, Khomeini retained a uniquely prominent position as Guide of the Revolution until his death. Article 107 of the constitution named him to the position for life, imposing election only after his death.

Ayatollah Ali Khamenei, 1989–present.

Supreme Leader Seyyed Ali Khamenei was preceded by Ayatollah Khomeini, the leader of Islamic Revolution in Iran. When Khomeini died, Khamenei was elected as the new Supreme Leader by the Assembly of Experts on June 4, 1989.

Electing an Islamic leader superior to all national and lawful organs is called Velayat e Faqih, first stated by Ayatollah Naraqi and expanded and revised by Ayatollah Khomeini. In this kind of leadership every decision is lawful only after approval of the supreme leader According to this theory, even democratic acts like national election of presidents which happens every four years in Iran are lawful only when the Supreme Leader signs his approval.

President of Iran is the head of government. The current president is Mahmoud Ahmadinejad.

The President of Iran is elected in a national election by universal adult suffrage — suffrage is extended to all over the age of 15. The selection of candidates for the election is restricted to those individuals approved by the 12-member religious Council of Guardians. The Councils members are appointed either directly or indirectly by the Supreme Leader and are intended to preserve the values of Irans theocratic Islamic government. To be eligible to run for president the Council proclaims the following qualifications be met:

- The candidate must be male (Disputed and currently debated)
- Be a Muslim
- Be between the ages of 25 and 75
- have no criminal record
- have no record of government service under the Iranian Monarchy
- be loyal to the Islamic Republic

Within these guidelines the Council vetoes candidates who are deemed unacceptable. The approval process is considered to be a check on the presidents power, and usually amounts to a very small minority of candidates being approved. In the 1997 election, for example, only four out of 238 presidential candidates were approved by the council. Western observers have routinely criticized the approvals process as a way for the Council and Supreme Leader to ensure that only conservative and like-minded Islamic fundamentalists can win office.

The President must be elected with a simple majority of the popular vote. A runoff election may be required to achieve this. The President serves for a term of four years and is eligible for a second term.

According to the Iranian constitution, When the President dies or is impeached, a special provisional *Presidential Council* temporarily rules in his place until an election can be held.

The President automatically becomes the Head of Council of Cultural Revolution and the Head of Council of National Security.

Presidents of Iran

- Abolhassan Banisadr - President from January 1980 (1980 election) to his impeachment in June of 1981.
- Mohammad Ali Rajai - elected president on August 2, 1981 (July 1981 election) in the wake of Banisadrs impeachment. Assassinated on August 30 of the same year.
- Ali Khamenei - elected president in October, 1981 (October 1981 election). Re-elected in 1985 (1985 election). Became Supreme Leader after the death of Ayatollah Khomeini in 1989. Fulfilled the role of both Supreme Leader and President between the death of Khomeini and the election of Rafsanjani.
- Ali Akbar Hashemi Rafsanjani - elected president in August of 1989 (1989 election), re-elected in 1993 (1993 election), served until August 1997.
- Mohammad Khatami - elected president in August of 1997 (1997 election), re-elected in 2001 (2001 election), served until August 2005.
- Mahmoud Ahmadinejad - elected in a runoff June 24, 2005 (2005 election), served since August 3, 2005.

Mahmoud Ahmadinejad transcribed into English as **Mahmud** or **Mahmood, Ahmadinezhad, Ahmadi-Nejad, Ahmadi Nejad, Ahmady Nejad**) (born October 28, 1956) is the current president of the Islamic Republic of Iran. He is a member of the Central Council of the Islamic Society of Engineers, but he has a more powerful base inside the Alliance of Builders of Islamic Iran (*Abadgaran*) and is considered one of the main figures in the alliance. Born in the village of Arādān near Garmsar, his family moved to Tehran when he was one year old. In 1976, he took Irans national university entrance exams to gain admission into Irans top universities. His test score ranked him 132nd among over 400,000 participants that year, landing him at the prestigious Elm Va Sanat University Of Tehran as an undergraduate student of civil engineering. He continued his studies and entered the Master of Science program for civil engineering in 1984. In 1987, he received his PhD in traffic and transportation engineering and planning. The graduate program was a special program for Revolutionary Guard members funded by the organization. After graduation, he was appointed a professor at the civil engineering department at IUST. Ahmadinejad is married, and has two sons and two daughters.

Guardian Council of the Constitution is an unelected high chamber within the constitution of the Islamic Republic of Iran. It has legislative, judicial, and electoral powers. This reflects the lack of separation of the branches of government in Iran. Guadian council represents the official will of the supreme leader.

Legislative functions

Bills are started in the Majlis; however, all bills must be reviewed and approved by the Guardian Council and to the

Expediency Council when they do not come to mutual agreement. The latter two chambers are low-profile entities, and, in spite of their overwhelming influence in lawmaking, have not received proportionate publicity. Another attestation of the power of the Guardian Council is that the Majlis has no legal status without the former.

The council also holds veto power over all legislation approved by the Majlis. It can nullify a law based on two accounts: being against Islamic laws, or being against the constitution. While all the members vote on the laws being compatible with the constitution, only the six clerics vote on them being compatible with Islam.

If any law is rejected, it will be passed back to the Majlis for correction. If the Majlis and the Council of Guardians cannot decide on a case, it is passed up to the Expediency Council for a final decision.

Judicial authority

The Council of Guardians also functions similar to a constitutional court. The authority to interpret the constitution is vested in the Council; interpretative decisions require a three-quarters majority of the Council. However, it does not conduct a court hearing where opposing sides are argued. Its deliberations are chiefly confidential.

Electoral authority

All candidates of parliamentary or presidential elections, as well as candidates for the Assembly of Experts, have to be qualified by the Guardian Council in order to run in the election. The Council is accorded supervision of elections.

The guardian council interpretes the term supervision in Article 99 as approbation supervision which implies the right for acceptance or rejection of elections legality and candidates competency. This interpretation is in contrast with the idea of notification supervision which does not imply the mentioned approval right.

Members

Its members are composed of Islamic clerics and lawyers. Six members of the Council are clerics selected by the Supreme Leader, who serves as Irans Head of State . The other six members are lawyers proposed by head of the judicial system of Iran (selected in turn by the Supreme Leader), and voted in by the Majlis Members are selected for six years on a phased basis, so that half the membership changes every three years.

The Supreme Leader has the power to dismiss the religious men of the Guardian Council

The current chairman of the council is Ayatollah Ahmad Jannati, deputized by the lawyer Abbasali Kadkhodai. Other cleric members are Sadegh Larijani, Mohammad Reza Modarresi-Yazdi, Mohammad Momen, Gholamreza Rezvani, and Mohammad Yazdi. The other lawyer members are Mohammad Reza Alizadeh, Ebrahim Azizi, Gholamhossein Elham (spokesman), Mohsen Esmaili, and Abbas Kabi.

Ahmad Jannati Massah (born in Esfahan in 1926) is an Iranian ayatollah and political figure. He is the leader of the Guardian Council, the body in charge of checking the

Majlis (Iranian parliament) with the Constitution of Iran and *sharia* (Islamic religious law) and approving the candidates in various elections. He is also a temporary Jumuah (Friday prayer) imam of Tehran.

He has been a member of the Guardian Council since 1980 and has been its chair since 1988.

Jannati is considered close to the Iranian Islamic conservatives, and is heavily criticized by the reformists for his active role in not approving reformist candidates to run in various elections and blocking their legislation.

He is disdainful of non-Muslims, having said non-Muslims are animals that chew their cud and cause corruption on Earth. During a Friday Prayer on 4 August 2006 Ayatollah Jannati asserted, Support for Hizbollah is a duty.

Ayatollah Jannati was one of the founders of Haghani School, one of the most influential religious school in Iran.

Majlis of Iran originally an Arabic word for (assembly), is a legislative body of Iran. The Majlis currently has 290 representatives, changed from the previous 270 seats since the February 18, 2000 election.

The current speaker of Majlis is Gholam Ali Haddad-Adel, with first deputy speaker Mohammad Reza Bahonar and second deputy speaker Mohammad Hassan Aboutorabi-Fard.

Before the Islamic Revolution, Majlis was also the name of the lower house of the Iranian Legislature from 1906 to 1979, the upper house being the Senate.

It was created by the Iran Constitution of 1906 and first convened on October 7, 1906, soon gaining power under the rule of the Mohammad Reza Pahlavi. Noteworthy bills passed by the Majlis under Pahlavi include the Oil Nationalization Bill

(March 15, 1951) and the Family Protection Law (1967), which gave women many basic rights such as custody of children in case of divorce. After the Iranian Revolution in 1979, the Senate was abolished and the National Consultative Assembly became the Islamic Consultative Assembly. Even though the Majlis has been known to voice opposition to both the Pahlavis and Islamic Republic policies, its power is not as great as that of the legislative bodies in the United States.

Women were not allowed to vote or be elected to the Majlis until 1963. This reform was opposed by some Islamic clerics, including Ayatollah Khomeini, who claimed that it was a plot to bring women to the public society, and out of the protection of the traditional family. The events led to a revolt on June 5, 1963 and the exile of Khomeini to Iraq. The twenty-first National Consultative Assembly, which included female representatives, opened on October 6, 1963.

Islamic Revolution

After the Islamic Revolution, when the Iranian legislature became unicameral.

From 1979, the Islamic Consultative Assembly had convened at the building that used to house the Iranian Senate, which is on Imam Khomeini Boulevard in central Tehran. A new building was built for the Assembly near Baharestan Square in central Tehran, near the old Majlis building that was used from 1906 to 1979. The move was considered and approved on October 9, 2001. Some Majlis representatives of the time voted against moving there, protesting the very high expenses. But the move didnt happen during the sixth Islamic Assembly, because of technical problems, include some related to the audio system.

The move was reconsidered by the representatives in the

seventh Islamic Assembly, in a private session on November 2, 2004, with the majority fraction divided over the issue and Emad Afrough, a conservative representative, calling the new building the Green Palace of Muawiyah (hinting that its too luxurious). But the move was finally approved with a good majority. The first session in new building was held on November 16, 2004.

Summary of the 20 February and 7 May 2004 Majlis of Iran election results

Orientiation of candidates	Votes	%	Seats
Conservatives			156
Reformists			39
Independents			31
Elected in second round			59
Armenians recognized minority religion			2
Chaldean and Assyrian Catholic recognized minority religion			1
Jewish recognized minority religion			1
Zoroastrian recognized minority religion			1
Total (Turnout around 50 %)			**290**

In an Iranian court the judge acts as prosecutor, jury, and arbiter; the system is a form of the inquisitorial system. However, according to Article 168 of Irans constitution, in certain cases involving the media a jury is allowed to be the arbiter. The judge holds absolute power. In practice, judges may be overwhelmed by cases, and not have the time to excogitate about each case. All judges are certified in Islamic law, and most, but not all, are members of the ruling clergy.

The lack of time and total control of the judge results in overcrowding in Iranian prisons.

The head of the **Judiciary** is appointed by the Supreme Leader, who in turn appoints the head of the Supreme Court and the chief public prosecutor.

Special courts

Public courts deal with civil and criminal cases. There are also Islamic Revolutionary Courts that try certain categories of offenses, including crimes against national security, narcotics smuggling, and acts that undermine the Islamic Republic. Decisions rendered in revolutionary courts are final and cannot be appealed.

The rulings of the Special Clerical Court , which functions independently of the regular judicial framework and is accountable only to the Supreme Leader, are also final and cannot be appealed. The Special Clerical Court handles crimes allegedly committed by clerics, although it has also taken on cases involving lay people.

Judicial system of Iran: The current judicial system was implemented and established by Ali Akbar Davar and some of his contemporaries. The system went through changes during the second Pahlavi era, and was drastically changed after the 1979 Revolution of Iran. Ever since then, the judicial system has been firmly based on Shia Islamic Law.

Contrary to expectation, matters pertaining to the constitution are decided by the Council of Guardians.

In an Iranian court the judge acts as prosecutor, jury, and arbiter; the system is a form of the inquisitorial system. However, according to Article 168 of Irans constitution, in certain cases involving the media a jury is allowed to be the arbiter. The judge holds absolute power. In practice, judges may be overwhelmed by cases, and not have the time to excogitate about each case. All judges are certified in Islamic law, and most, but not all, are members of the ruling clergy.

The lack of time and total control of the judge results in overcrowding in Iranian prisons.

The head of the **Judiciary** is appointed by the Supreme Leader, who in turn appoints the head of the Supreme Court and the chief public prosecutor.

Special courts

Public courts deal with civil and criminal cases. There are also Islamic Revolutionary Courts that try certain categories of offenses, including crimes against national security, narcotics smuggling, and acts that undermine the Islamic Republic. Decisions rendered in revolutionary courts are final and cannot be appealed.

The rulings of the Special Clerical Court , which functions independently of the regular judicial framework and is accountable only to the Supreme Leader, are also final and cannot be appealed. The Special Clerical Court handles crimes allegedly committed by clerics, although it has also taken on cases involving lay people.

Human rights in Iran

Today, the state of **human rights by the Islamic Republic of Iran** continues to be generally considered a source of significant concern. Despite many efforts by Iranian human right activists, writers, NGOs and international critiques as well as several resolutions by the UN General Assembly and the UN Human Rights Commission, the government of Iran continues to restrict freedom of speech, gender equality and other forms of freedom.

Furthermore, the Islamic regime of Iran still continues to disregard the Universal Declaration of Human Rights in several aspects.

Iran has been rated by several human rights groups as one of todays leading abusers of human rights, whose leaders repeatedly remove any sort of freedom including even those granted by basic human existence.

Death penalty

According to Amnesty Internationals 2004 report, at least 108 people were executed that year, most of whom having been political prisoners. Amnesty has also described cases in which adolescent children were sentenced to the death penalty. Though officially illegal, torture is often carried out in Iranian prisons, as in the widely publicized case of photojournalist Zahra Kazemi.

Like 74 other countries in the world, Iran carries out capital punishment. As a State party to the International Convention on Civil and Political Rights (ICCPR) and the Convention on the Rights of the Child (CRC), Iran has undertaken not to execute anyone for an offence committed when they were under the age of 18, but continues to carry such executions out, and is one of only six nations in the world to do so. According to Article 6 of the ICCPR, Sentence of death shall not be imposed for crimes committed by persons below eighteen years of age.

Assembly of Experts (also **Assembly of Experts for the Leadership**) of Iran *Majles-e-Khobregan* or *Majles-e-Khebregan*), is a congressional body of 86 Ayatollahs which selects the Supreme Leader and supervises his activities. Members of the assembly are elected by direct public vote to eight year terms. The next term (4th term) however will exceptionally last ten years due to the election aggregation plan of Iran in order that the government can run one simultaneous election for both Assembly of Experts and Parliament and economize in the election costs.

Functions

According to the Iranian Constitution, the assembly is in charge of supervising, dismissing and electing the Supreme Leader, who is then appointed for life. However the assembly has the power to remove him at any time. The assembly gathers every six months and elects a new Supreme Leader, in the event of dismissal or death of the previous Supreme Leader.

The constitution does not have any requirements with regards to the members of the assembly, and leaves the assembly itself in charge of requirements and vetting candidates. The assembly has passed laws to require all its members be experts in Fiqh (Islamic jurisprudence), so they are able to judge the activities of the Supreme Leader, and making sure he does not violate Islamic rules and is complying to his duties according to the constitution. This law is being challenged by the Reformists, and their 2006 election campaign includes changing this law to allow non-clerics into the assembly, and reversing the law that allows Guardian Council to vet candidates.

The members are elected by public vote for eight-year terms. The candidates are subject to approval of the Guardian Council. Currently, the average age of its members is over 60 years, which results in many mid-term elections. The next election is due to take place December 15, 2006. The meetings and the meeting notes of the assembly are confidential.

Supreme National Security Council is the National Security Council of the Islamic Republic of Iran, the current chair whereof is Ali Larijani. This institution was founded during the 1989 revision of the Constitution.

Composition

This National Security Council is mandated by Article 176 of the Constitution of the Islamic Republic of Iran to be presided over by the president of the country. The Supreme Leader — the de facto president of this Council — is supposed to be the final decider of conclusions. Nevertheless, the council has recently been presided over by Hassan Rowhani and Ali Larijani in lieu of the president.

Ministry of Intelligence and National Security is the primary intelligence agency of the Islamic Republic of Iran. It is also known as **SAVAMA** and **VEVAK**. It is an important part of the Iranian governments security apparatus, and is well funded and equipped. Before a thorough overhaul of the organization in 1998 under President Mohammad Khatami which took place after the famous scandal of the serial murders of writers, the organization had been accused of being involved in terrorist activities, including assassination of Iranian political dissidents inside and outside the country and training and funding Hezbollah.

History

Information on the ministry **of Intelligence and National Security** is often difficult to obtain. The organization was intended to replace SAVAK, Irans intelligence agency during the rule of the Shah, but it is unclear how much continuity there is between the two organizations—while their role is similar, their underlying ideology is radically different. It is suspected that the new government was initially eager to purge SAVAK elements from the new organization, but that pragmatism eventually prevailed, with many experienced SAVAK personnel being retained in their roles. Former SAVAK staff are believed to have been important in the ministrys infiltration of left-wing dissident groups and of the Iraqi Baath Party.

The formation of the ministry was proposed by Saeed Hajjarian to the government of Mir-Hossein Mousavi and then the parliament. There were debates about which branch of the state should oversee the new institution, and the other options apart from the presidency were the Judiciary system, the Supreme Leader, and Islamic Revolutionary Guards Corps. Finally, the government could get the approval of Ayatollah Khomeini to make it a ministry, but a restriction was added to the requirements of the minister, needing him to be a *mujtahid*.

The ministry was finally founded on August 18, 1984, abandoning many small intelligence agencies that were formed in different governmental organizations. The five ministers since the founding of the ministry, have been Mohammad Reyshahri (under Prime Minister Mir-Hossein Mousavi), Ali Fallahian (under President Ali Akbar Hashemi Rafsanjani), Ghorbanali Dorri-Najafabadi (under President Mohammad Khatami, resigned after a year), Ali Younessi (under President Khatami, until August 24, 2005), and Gholam Hossein Mohseni-Ejehei (under President Mahmoud Ahmadinejad, from August 24, 2005).

Government of Iran is headed by Iranian President Mahmoud Ahmadinejad. However, the ultimate head of Irans political establishment is the Supreme Leader, who is a religious figure elected by the Assembly of Experts.

Controversy

According to current election laws, a body of 12 experts called the Guardian Council oversees and approves electoral candidates for most national elections in Iran. Half of the members of this body are appointed by the Supreme Leader. According to the current law, this council vets also Assembly of Experts candidates, which in turn in supervise and elect the Supreme Leader, which ultimately creates a closed loop of power.

In addition, current elections law requires Assembly of Experts candidates to be religious mujtahids, which greatly narrows the potential field.

Neither of these two laws are mandated by the constitution and are *ordinary* laws passed by the Parliament or the Assembly of Experts, which therefore can theoretically be reversed. However, despite efforts of many political activists, it has proven to be practically impossible to do so until now.

Many Iranian reformists (including Abdollah Noori) consider this to be the core legal obstacle for a truly democratic system in Iran.

The president of the republic is elected by universal suffrage to a four-year term by an absolute majority of votes and is the head of the executive branch. The president appoints and supervises the Council of Ministers (members of the cabinet), coordinates government decisions, and selects government policies to be placed before the Islamic Assembly (Parliament). According to the constitution, the President is the *head of government* and is emphasized as the highest ranking official in the country after the Supreme Leader. The President is in charge of enforcing the constitution and supervising the proper execution of its laws except for matters directly stated as duties of the Supreme Leader in the constitution.

Political parties in Iran.

Iran is a state with regular presidential and parliamentary elections. The system as a whole is presently is a republic based on Islamic fundamentalists. Local elections have taken place in 1999 and 2003. A limited number of opposition parties are allowed, but are widely considered to have no real chance of gaining power.

7777777777777777777

The parties

It is quite difficult to get a clear view on Iranian political parties. There are not opposition parties in Iran as all must make commitment to absolute rule by the Supreme Leader.

Parties and groups

Conservative:

Militant Clergy Association: secretary-general Mohammad Reza Mahdavi-Kani

Islamic Coalition Party : secretary-general Habibollah Asgarowladi

Association of Islamic Revolution Loyalists : secretary-general Hasan Ghaffuri-Fard

Moderation and Development Party : secretary-general Mohammad Baqer Nowbakht

Etelaf-e Khedmatgozaran-e Mostaqel-e Iran : spokesman Emad Afruq

Iranian Nations Welfare Party : secretary-general Khalil Ali Mohammadzadeh

Reformist

In 1999, 18 political groups announced the formation of the 2 Khordad Front (23 May Front, a reference to the date of President Khatamis election in 1997). The aim was to adopt a unified strategy and to field the greatest number of joint candidates in the 2000 elections.

It includes:

- Militant Clerics Society : secretary-general Mohammad Mousavi Khoeiniha
- Islamic Iran Participation Front : secretary-general Mohammad Reza Khatami, outgoing deputy majlis speaker, presidents brother
- National Confidence Party : secretary-general Mehdi Karrubi (outgoing majlis speaker)
- Executives of Construction Party : secretary-general Gholamhoseyn Karbaschi, former mayor of Tehran
- Society of Forces Following the Line of the Imam : secretary-general Hadi Khamenei (supreme leaders brother)
- Organisation of the Mojahedin of the Islamic Revolution : secretary-general Mohammad Salamati
- Islamic Labour Party : secretary-general Abolqasem Sarhadizadeh, outgoing deputy for Tehran
- Workers House : secretary-general Alireza Mahjub, outgoing deputy for Tehran
- Islamic Iran Solidarity Party : secretary-general Ebrahim Asgharzadeh
- There are also a few non-allowed opposition groups like the Freedom Movement Party of Ebrahim Yazdi and the National Religious Forces of Ezatollah Sahabi.

Opposition parties active in exile :

There are roughly 40 parties outside Iran which can be divided between 5 ideological branches :
-   the Communists
-   the Social-Democrats
-   the Muslim-Democrats
-   the Republican Nationalists
-   the Monarchist Nationalists

What is important is that a lot of Iranians dont know the majority of these 40 exiled political parties. The parties known by all Iranians are Peoples Mujahedin of Iran, the Monarchists, the National Front, the Fadayan-e Khalq and the Tudeh Party (considered by many to be the true Communist Party). For example, few Iranians are aware of the existence of the Hekmatist Party although the latter is well active outside Iran. Only 5 parties out of the 40 could be considered powerful, in order :

- the **Peoples Mujahedin of Iran** of Maryam Rajavi, (Conservative)

- the **Constitutionalist Party of Iran** of Reza Pahlavi, (Democrat-Liberal)

- the **United Republicans of Iran**, (Social-Democratic) linked with the the **Organisation of Iranian Peoples Fedaian (Majority)**, (Socialist)

- the **National Front of Iran**, (Center-Left)

- the **Hekmatist Party** of Koorosh Modaressi, (Communist).

Only a union of the five parties cited above could be considered representative of the whole exiled Opposition parties. There are important individuals with no party who are also important : Ali Afshari, Amir Abbas Fakhravar or Manuchehr Mohammadi from the student segment, Mohsen Sazegara, a founder of Irans Revolutionary Guards, Roya Tolouee, a woman activist, Akbar Ganji, Abbas Amir-Entezam, the longest political prisoner of Iran (27 years), etc.

The rest of the Opposition is insignificant, for example the Labor Party, or the Green Party, or the Liberal Democratic Party, etc, are more very little associations than politial parties. But some are bigger to other ones:

- The **Tudeh Party** and the **Komalah**, which were important parties in the past, exist in a very anemic state.

- The **National Movement of Iranian Resistance** of Shahpour Bakhtiar and the **PDKI** of Abdul Rahman Qasimlo, although prominent parties in the past, have almost been destroyed with the killings of their charismatic leaders by the Islamic Republic.

- The new **Marze Por Gohar Party** is still too small, too localized and unknown inside Iran.

There are news that since September 2005 some of these exiled parties who used to be very divided (even among groups of similar philosophies) have begun to unite.

A lot of parties tried to unite in the past and failed. Very few succeeded like the National Council of Resistance of Iran and the Workers Left Unity - Iran but they were (and are) only a union of two parties : the conservative *Peoples Mujahedin of Iran* and the marxist *Organisation of Iranian People Fadaee Guerillas* for the first one and the *Iranian fedaian communist league* and the *Organisation of*

Revolutionary Workers of Iran (Rahe Kargar) for the latter.

Since 2003 the pro-republican (mostly leftist) activists did what no others had done in the past : they created the United Republicans of Iran, a federation of pro-republican parties.

But more importantly, a huge gathering of all important iranian parties and activists (including the monarchists and rightist parties like the Pan-Iranist Party) called Neshaste Landan took place in London for the first time in June 2006.

Before, some discussions had been held in Paris (Neshaste Paris) and later in Berlin (Neshaste Berlin). Since that time, cooperation and dialogue between them has accelerated. For the first time, a Republican (the spokesman of the National Front of Iran) Parviz Varjavand wrote in an article in August 2006 that Democracy is compatible with both a Constitutional Monarchy and a Republic and that the issue is not between Constitutional Monarchy and Republic. The Green Party of Iran led by Kayvan Koboli said the same thing months before Parviz Varjavand . Recently, Heshmat Raeisi, ex-member of the Central Committee of both the Fedai and the Tudeh Party participated in the sixth Congress of the Constitutionalist Party of Iran in November 2006 and gave a speech .

This Neshaste Landan has been considered historical in the history of the Iranian Opposition by all political tendencies and has a special site : http://neshastelondon.info

But it hasnt produced any results until now. And the name of all the parties which took part in this gathering is not known.

Here are the names and the programs of all known iranian political parties based in exile (Europe, USA, Canada, Australia, and sometimes Turkey, Iraq, Dubai, Israel) :

The Communists

There are 16 iranian communist parties. However only three out of them could be considered active, namely the Hekmatist Party, the Organisation of Iranian Peoples Fedaian (Majority) and the Komalah.

The well-known Communist Party which used to be very powerful. No longer very active.Tudeh Party of Iran led by Ali Khavari.

Foreign relations of Iran

Ayatollah Khomeinis revolutionary regime initiated sharp changes from the foreign policy pursued by the Shah, particularly in reversing the countrys orientation toward the West. Following Irans initial post-revolutionary idealistic and hard-line foreign policy and the Iran-Iraq war, the country has begun to settle down into a more rational foreign policy. However, this is still occasionally overshadowed by rhetoric.

In recent years Iran has made great strides in improving relations with its neighbours, particularly Saudi Arabia. Irans regional goals are trying not to be dominated by wanting to establish a leadership role, curtail the presence of the United States and other outside powers, and build trade ties. In broad terms, Irans foreign policy emphasizes three main guidelines:

It takes stances against the United States and Israel, the former as a military power that threatens it in the Persian Gulf, and the latter as part of its stance to support the Palestinians.

It wants to eliminate outside influence in the region. Iran sees itself as a regional power, when global powers such as the United States or the United Kingdom do not supersede it. It seeks to reduce their presence in the Persian Gulf wherever possible.

It pursues a great increase in diplomatic contacts with developing and non-aligned countries, as part of an effort to build trade and political support, now that it has lost its pre-revolutionary US backing.

Despite these guidelines, however, bilateral relations are frequently confused and contradictory, due to Irans oscillation between pragmatic and ideological concerns.

US - Iran relations

Political relations between **Iran and the United States** began when the Shah of Persia, Nassereddin Shah Qajar, officially dispatched Persias first ambassador, Mirza Abolhasan Shirazi to Washington D.C. in the mid to late 1800s. In 1883, Samuel Benjamin was appointed by the United States as the first official diplomatic envoy to Iran.

Persia and the United States were political and cultural allies until the post-World War II era. Until 1979, they remained political allies, but after a series of conflicts and incidents between the two nations, tension developed in their relationship.

Even before political relations, since the early to mid 1880s, Americans had been traveling to Iran. Justin Perkins and Asahel Grant were the first missionaries to be dispatched to Persia in 1834 via the American Board of Commissioners for Foreign Missions.

The famous vizier of Nasereddin Shah, Amir Kabir, also initiated direct contacts with Americans when he signed an agreement with the United States to establish a Navy base in Bushehr to help create a Navy force for Persia.Urmia Universitys College of Medicine, is another example of prediplomatic relations between Persia and the United States; the university was founded by a group of American physicians in the 1870s.

By the end of the 19th century, negotiations were underway for an American company to establish a railway system from the Persian Gulf to Tehran. In 1901, an American Company based in Buffalo, New York, officially requested Persias government to send an envoy to Buffalo for assessment of its exhibit for the project. The project never materialized, presumably under British pressure.

Up until WW2, relations between Iran and the United States remained cordial. As a result many constitutionalist Iranians came to view the U.S. as a third force in their struggle to break free of the humiliating British and Russian meddling and dominance in Persian affairs. As a result of this trust, beginning from the second parliament, Irans government appointed Americans as Treasury General of Persia three times. The posts were held by: Arthur Millspaugh, Morgan Shuster, and Elgin Groseclose. It is even believed that such appointments were the result of contacts made by the Persian Constitutional revolutionaries with the executive branch of the US government, even though no official documents of such contacts exist. What is certain however is that Persias drive for modernizing its economy and liberating it from British and Russian influences had the full support of American industrial and business leaders. During the Persian Constitutional Revolution, Howard Baskerville died in Tabriz when trying to help the constitutionalists, and after Morgan Shuster was appointed Treasury General of Persia, an American was killed in Tehran by henchmen thought to be affiliated with Russian or British interests. Shuster became even more active in supporting the Constitutional revolution of Persia financially. When *Shua al-Saltaneh* the Shahs brother who was aligned with the goals of Imperial Russia in Persia, was ordered by Irans government to surrender his assets to it, Shuster was assigned this task, which he promptly moved to execute. Imperial Russia immediately landed troops in Bandar Anzali demanding a recourse and apology from the Persian government. Eventually, Irans parliament in Tehran was shelled by General Liakhoff of Imperial Russia, and the American Morgan Shuster was forced to resign under tremendous British and Russian pressure. Shusters book *The Strangling of Persia* is a recount of the details of these events, a harsh criticism of Britain and Imperial Russia. It was the American embassy that first relayed to the Iran desk at the Foreign Office in London confirmation of the popular view that the British were involved in the 1921 coup that brought Reza Pahlavi to power. A British Embassy report from 1932 admits that the British put Reza Shah on the throne. The United States was not an ally of Britain as far as Persia was concerned at that point in time. Morgan Shuster was soon to be followed by Arthur Millspaugh, appointed as Treasury General by Reza Shah Pahlavi, and Arthur Pope, who was a main driving force behind the *Persian Empire* revivalist policies of Reza Shah. But the friendly relations between the United States and Iran were about to change at the onset of the 1950s.

Politics of oil, a turning point

From 1952-53, Irans democratically elected nationalist Prime Minister Mohammed Mossadeq began a period of rapid power consolidation, which led the Shah, Mohammad Reza Pahlavi, to a brief exile and then into power again. Much of the events of 1952 were started by Mossadeqs nationalization of the Anglo-Iranian Oil Company, now

British Petroleum. Established by the British in the early 20th century, an agreement had been made to share profits (85% British-15% Iran), but the company withheld their financial records from the Iranian government. Due to alleged profit monopolization by the Anglo-Iranian Oil company, the Iranian Parliament had unanimously agreed to nationalize its holding of, what was at the time, the British Empires largest company.

The United States and Britain, through a now-admitted covert operation of the CIA called Operation Ajax, conducted from the US Embassy in Tehran, helped organize protests to overthrow Moussadeq and return the Shah to Iran. The operation failed and the Shah fled to Italy. After a second successful operation he returned from his brief exile. Irans fledgling attempts at democracy quickly descended into dictatorship, as the Shah dismantled the constitutional limitations on his office and began to rule as an absolute monarch.

During his reign, the Shah received significant American support, frequently making state visits to the White House and earning praise from numerous American Presidents. The Shahs close ties to Washington and his bold agenda of rapidly Westernizing Iran soon began to infuriate certain segments of the Iranian population, especially the hardline Islamic conservatives.

Prior to the Iranian Revolution of 1979, Iran had one of the worlds largest number of students residing in the United States.

In 1979, the Iranians revolted and the Shah was ousted for a second time. Ayatollah Khomeni became Irans new leader and soon began issuing vicious rhetoric against the United States, describing the country as the Great Satan and a nation of infidels.

The American administration under President Jimmy Carter refused to give the Shah any further support and expressed no interest in attempting to return him to power. A significant embarrassment for Carter occurred when the Shah, as of that time suffering from cancer, requested entry into the United States for treatment. Carter reluctantly agreed, but the move only reinforced Iranian notions that the former monarch was an American puppet

Iran-Russia relations

During the Iran-Iraq war, the USSR supplied Saddam Hussein with large amounts of conventional arms. Ayatollah Khomeini deemed Islam principally incompatible with the communist ideals of the Soviet Union, leaving the secular Saddam as an ally of Moscow.

After the war, especially with the fall of the USSR, Tehran-Moscow relations witnessed a sudden increase in diplomatic and commercial relations, and Iran soon even began purchasing weapons from Russia.

By the mid 1990s, Russia had already agreed to continue work on developing Irans Nuclear Program, with plans to finish constructing the nearly 20 year delayed Nuclear Reactor plant of Bushehr.

Iran in turn, a self-proclaimed advocate of Muslim national rights (such as in Lebanon and Palestine), was largely silent in condemning the violence against Chechnya during the first and second Chechen Wars

In 2005, Russia was the seventh largest trading partner of Iran, with 5.33% of all exports to Iran originating from Russia. Trade relations between the two exceed USD$1 billion.

As confrontation between the United States and the European Union on one side and Iran on the other escalates, Tehran is finding itself further pushed into an alliance with Beijing and Moscow. And Iran, like Russia, views Turkeys regional ambitions and the possible spread of some form of pan-Turkic ideology with suspicion.

Russia and Iran also share a common interest in limiting the political influence of the United States in Central Asia. This common interest has led the Shanghai Cooperation Organization to extend to Iran observer status in 2005, and offer full membership in 2006. Irans relations with the organization, which is dominated by Russia and China, represents the most extensive diplomatic ties Iran has shared since the 1979 revolution.

The solidity of Tehran-Moscow ties remains to be seen and tested however. Russia is increasingly becoming dependent on its economic relations with the West, and is thus gradually becoming vulnerable to western pressures in trying to curb its ties with Tehran. Iran has also expressed its unhappiness with the repeated delays by Russia in finishing the Bushehr Reactor project, as well as Russias stance in the Caspian Sea dispute. Many experts regard the ties as not even serving mutual interests:

Russian-Iranian relations are driven by Russian interests, rather than mutual goals.

Unlike previous years in which Irans air fleet were entirely western made, Irans Air Force and civilian air fleet are increasingly becoming Russian built as the US and Europe continues to maintain sanctions on Iran.

China- Iran relations

Chinas missile trade and cooperation with Iran has been a subject of substantial proliferation concern in Washington since the 1980s. The Chinese helped on the part of the Fuel

Cycle that involved in making Uranium Hexafluoride, this is the gas that is fed into the Centrifuge. They were going to build a facility under contract for the Iraninans. Under strong pressure from United State government China looked at the financial ledgers and realized that it was making a lot more money from its trade with the United States than it would from helping Iran. China decided to completely terminate their involvement with this facility, but it continued help in other areas. Chinas missile exports and assistance to Iran have generally fallen into two areas: the provision of anti-ship cruise missiles and related technology, and technical assistance for Irans ballistic missile program, as well as some exports of complete ballistic missiles. Washington fears that Chinese ballistic and cruise missile exports and assistance to Iran could provide the material and technical base for Iranian development and deployment of missiles that could be used in the delivery of weapons of mass destruction. Irans growing military capability, of which the missile program forms an important part, could raise regional tensions in the Persian Gulf, and directly threaten US interests in the region, especially the safe passage of oil tankers, as well as the security interests of US allies in the region, such as Israel. Disputes over Chinese missile exports and assistance to Iran have impeded bilateral relations and undermined the bases for US-China cooperation in other areas of mutual and global concern.

In reaction to US pressure, China took specific steps to stem its missile exports and assistance to Iran, including suspension of sales of the C-801/802 cruise missiles. This progress coincided with the US-China summits in 1997-1998. To a large extent these initial concessions by the Chinese were part of a broader Chinese strategic thrust where compromises in these issue areas were intended to pave the way for achieving significant results in others. In the past, China implicitly linked its MTCR commitments to issues of increasing salience to its own security concerns, namely, ballistic missile defense and US arms sales to Taiwan. However, in the last few years, Chinas increasing acceptance of international arms control and nonproliferation norms, and growing dependence on imported energy has made Beijing increasingly concerned about the stability of the Middle East.

Although the summit diplomacy of 1997 and 1998 improved cooperation between Washington and Beijing for a time, US-China relations deteriorated significantly in the last year of the Clinton administration and the first year of the Bush presidency. This downturn in the relationship was precipitated by a number of events, including the NATO bombing of the Chinese embassy, the release of the Cox Report, the growing tension over the Taiwan issue, passage in the House of the Taiwan Security Enhancement Act, and the EP-3 spy plane incident. In this period, bilateral cooperation in arms control and nonproliferation stagnated.

Bilateral relations improved once again, however, after the September 11th attacks in the United States, and cooperation between Washington and Beijing has since increased. In reaction to U.S. pressure and a recognition of the threat that proliferation of WMD has on Chinas national security, Beijing released a comprehensive set of export controls in 2002. Although not entirely addressing U.S. concerns about transfers to Iran, the new export controls went far in strengthening Chinas control on exports of missile related technology. Recent US sanctions against Chinese firms indicate that despite evident progress in Chinese export controls, US officials are still not satisfied with Beijings efforts at controlling the spread of WMD and missile technology.

Since the early 1980s, Chinese arms transfers were

increasingly driven by commercial considerations. With declining defense budgets, the various defense industrial sectors were under tremendous pressure to turn to consumer goods production and try to market military products abroad. Indeed, the need to earn foreign currency may have been the single most important factor motivating Chinese military exports, including missiles. This export-push is clearly evident in the space industry. Facing severe financial difficulties due to insufficient domestic military orders and a two-thirds cut in R&D appropriations in the early 1980s, industry officials were forced to come up with plans to make up for the short-falls. Indeed, the designing and developing of the M-series missiles in large measures were a practical response to the financial crunch.

China first began exporting missiles to Iran in 1985, during the Iran-Iraq war, when China supplied weapons and military technology to both sides. In 1986-1987, China reportedly transferred HY-2 (Silkworm) anti-ship cruise missiles to Iran, causing the United States to issue a protest to Beijing and to temporarily freeze liberalization of high technology exports to China. In 1989, China also sold around 150-200 M-7/8610 ballistic missiles to Iran, and began providing Iran with production technology for an indigenous ballistic missile, the Iran-130. Throughout this period, China denied that it had directly supplied missiles to Iran or Iraq, stating that Chinese arms were available on the international market, and criticized the US for spreading rumors about Chinas arms sales.

Evidence surfaced again in the early 1990s that China was directly providing Iran with production technology, equipment, training, and testing facilities for the indigenous Iranian manufacture of Chinese-designed HY-2 anti-ship missiles as well as for ballistic missiles, particularly at the Isfahan missile facility in Iran. Some reports indicated that the transfer of missile guidance technology might violate Missile Technology Control Regime (MTCR) guidelines, but there was no real discussion from the US government about imposing sanctions. Some in Washington worried that Iran would use Chinese missiles as delivery systems for nuclear weapons, should Iran succeed in developing them. China also reportedly assisted Irans efforts to upgrade its North Korean Scud missiles, and has also supplied technical and manufacturing assistance to a number of indigenous Iranian missile programs, including the Iran-130 (a.k.a. Mushak-120), Iran-700, NP-110, and Zelzal-3. China continued to vigorously deny that it was supplying ballistic missile technology to Iran.

A 1995 CIA report suggested some Chinese transfers of missile technology to Iran might have violated MTCR guidelines, which would require US sanctions. However, no sanctions were ever imposed for the transfers, largely because the evidence was inconclusive. The possibility of sanctions was again raised in 1996, when media reports stated China had transferred advanced C-802 anti-ship cruise missiles to Iran, which could trigger US sanctions under the 1992 Iran-Iraq Nonproliferation Act. US officials decided, however, that the number and type of weapons transferred were not destabilizing and thus did not meet the legal requirement for sanctions. In 1996, China reportedly began assisting Iran in developing indigenous anti-ship cruise missiles, based on Chinese designs. According to another CIA report, China and Iran signed a $3 billion deal in August 1996 that included the sale of Chinese ballistic missiles, missile guidance technology (including sensitive gyroscopes), and missile production equipment. When the contents of the CIA report appeared in the US media in October 1996, China called the report fictitious and not worth refuting. US State Department officials at the time indicated that they believed Beijing was generally operating within the nonproliferation assurances it had given Washington.

The CIAs 1997 report to Congress stated that China continued to help Irans missile programs. According to this report: The Chinese provided a tremendous variety of assistance to both Irans and Pakistans ballistic missile programs during the second half of 1996. Much of this assistance continued for a number of years, mainly in the form of missile technologies for Irans short-range, MTCR-compliant missile programs which can also be used for longer range systems.

However, under US pressure, China began to curb its missile cooperation with Iran. In September 1997, Chinese Foreign Minister Qian Qichen informally pledged to US Secretary of State Madeleine Albright that China would halt its new sales of cruise missiles to Iran. This pledge reportedly included the cruise missile production technologies as well. On 20 January 1998, US Defense Secretary William Cohen had received personal assurances from Chinese President Jiang Zemin and Defense Minister Chi Haotian that China has halted all transfers of anti-ship cruise missiles to Iran, and that Beijing would not assist Iran in upgrading its current cruise missile inventory. Cohen stated that It was the very clear message that no sales will go forward, no transfers--period--to Iran. That would include those missiles that have been contracted for before. Cohen stated that Defense Minister Chi had reiterated assurances that cruise missile sales to Iran had ceased, saying, I believe that we have assurances that such sales will not continue in the future...I am satisfied that there will not be a contribution to the kind of conventional weaponry that would jeopardize American ships in the [Persian] Gulf. In 2002, China published a comprehensive set of export controls, for the most part coinciding with the MTCR. The Bush administration welcomed this development, but chose to take a wait and see approach about Chinas compliance with nonproliferation pledges. Since the publishing of these export controls, Chinese companies have been sanctioned three times for missile related sales to Iran. Although official US statements on these sanctions have been short on detail, the items in question appeared to be dual-use items not covered by the MTCR.

Chinese assistance has played a key role in the Irans missile development, with Chinese exports and assistance dating back twenty years. For the United States, missile proliferation to Iran undermines international nonproliferation efforts, heightens regional tension, especially in the oil-rich Persian Gulf region, and directly threatens US access to oil supplies, and potentially threatens regional allies such as Israel. The US has identified Iran as one of the most active rogue states engaging in the acquisitions of weapons of mass destruction and their delivery systems. In 2002, George W. Bush included Iran in the Axis of Evil. Given US security interests, preventing Iran from obtaining items, technologies, and assistance for its WMD and missile development programs has been a top priority to US policy makers. In the US-China context, these issues also demonstrate continued differences between Washington and Beijing on missile threats and the MTCR regime. Recent moves by Beijing indicate that China increasingly recognizes the proliferation of WMD and missile technology as a direct threat to its own national security. However many in Washington are still concerned that Beijing is not consistently implementing its nonproliferation policies. According to a statement in 2003 by Assistant Secretary of State Paula DeSutter: Chinese officials at every level have said both publicly and privately to us that China recognizes the importance of this issue, however the United States government continues to see problems in the proliferant behavior of certain Chinese entities and remain deeply concerned about the Chinese governments often narrow interpretation of nonproliferation commitments and lack of enforcement of nonproliferation regulations.

China has its own security concerns regarding the various nonproliferation regimes, which are reflected in Beijings positions on MTCR compliance and missile transfer issues. China has primarily expressed concern about three critical issues. First is the regimes discriminatory nature regarding controlled items and its failure to address the demand side of missile proliferation. Beijing argued in the past that ballistic missiles per se are not weapons of mass destruction, but rather delivery vehicles just like high-performance fighter aircraft, which are also capable of carrying nuclear, biological, and chemical weapons. Indeed, the Chinese have not consider missiles with conventional warheads as inherently destabilizing, as they are not as effective as high-performance strike aircraft (in terms of accuracy, ability to hit mobile targets, etc). Chinese officials had suggested previously that the MTCR be revised to cover the latter as well. Second, China has been critical of a double standard in MTCR implementation, arguing that the regime did not prohibit missile proliferation between member states. US missile defense plans have only reinforced Beijings views in this regard. Beijing views Washingtons intention to incorporate Japan and Taiwan into its missile defense system as a form of missile proliferation since it is difficult to distinguish between defensive and offensive application of the missile technology. Finally, Chinas regional security concerns, in particular the opposition to arms sales to Taiwan and missile defenses to Taiwan and Japan, have convinced Beijings leadership that Washington only cares its own absolute security without consideration of others interests. Chinese officials have previously complained that Beijing has already made a number of concessions, such as suspending nuclear cooperation with Iran and stopping delivery of C-802 cruise missiles, yet claim that China has received little in return from the United States.

Iran-Israel relations

Relations between Iran and Israel have alternated from close political alliances between the two states during the era of the Pahlavi dynasty to hostility following the rise to power of Ayatollah Ruhollah Khomeini. Currently, the countries do not have diplomatic relations with each other. Iran does not even formally recognize Israel as a country, and official government texts often simply refer to it as the Zionist entity or the zionist regime.

The history of the Persian Jews has been uninterrupted for over 2,500 years. It is a Mizrahi Jewish community in the territory of todays Iran, the historical core of the former Persian Empire, which began as early as the 8th century BCE, at the time of captivity of the ancient Israelites in Khorasan.

As of 2005, Iran has the largest Jewish population in the Middle East outside of Israel. A larger population of Iranian Jews reside in Israel with the President of Israel Moshe Katsav, the former Chief of Staff / Defense Minister Shaul Mofaz, current Chief of staff Dan Halutz and Israeli hip-hop star Kobi Shimoni (Subliminal) being the most famous of this group.

Upon its establishment in 1948 and until the Iranian Revolution in 1979, Israel enjoyed cordial relations with Iran (then ruled by the Pahlavi dynasty). Iran was one of the first nations to internationally recognize Israel, and was considered one of Israels closest and few Muslim friends (Israel has maintained a stable partnership with Turkey, as well). In spite of this, Iran voted in support of the UN General Assembly Resolution 3379 in 1975 which equated Zionism with racism (the resolution, however, was later revoked with Resolution 4686 in 1991, which Iran voted against. However, Iran and Israel did develop close military ties during this period. This can be seen from the development of joint venture military projects, such as Project Flower, the Iranian-Israeli attempt to develop a new missile. For details on Irans strategic reasoning during the 1970s, see Israel and the Origins of Irans Arab Option: Dissection of a Strategy Misunderstood, Middle East Journal, Volume 60, Number 3, Summer 2006.

It was Ayatollah Khomeini who first declared Israel as an enemy of Islam during the second Pahlavi period in his campaign against Shah Mohammad Reza Pahlavi, who supported Israel.

After the second phase of the 1979 Iranian Revolution which witnessed the establishment of the Islamic Republic, Iran withdrew its recognition of the state of Israel and cut off all official relations.

Will Iran use nukes against Isreal

One of Irans most influential ruling cleric called on the Muslim states to use nuclear weapon against Israel, assuring them that while such an attack would annihilate

Israel, it would cost them damages only.

If a day comes when the world of Islam is duly equipped with the arms Israel has in possession, the strategy of colonialism would face a stalemate because application of an atomic bomb would not leave any thing in Israel but the same thing would just produce damages in the Muslim world, Ayatollah Ali Akbar Hashemi-Rafsanjani told the crowd at the traditional Friday prayers in Tehran. Mr. Hashemi-Rafsanjanis speech was the strongest against Israel, but also this is the first time that a prominent leader of the Islamic Republic openly suggests the use of nuclear weapon against the Jewish State.

While Israel is believed to possess between 100 to 200 nuclear war heads, the Islamic Republic and Iraq are known to be working hard to produce their own atomic weapons with help from Russia and North Korea, Pakistan, also a Muslim state, has already a certain number of nuclear bomb.

In a lengthy speech to mark the so-called International Qods (Jerusalem) Day celebrated in Iran only, Mr. Hashemi-Rafsanjani, who, as the Chairman of the **Assembly to Discern the Interests of the State,** is the Islamic Republics number two man after Ayatollah Ali Khamenehi, said since Israel was an emanation of Western colonialism therefore in future it will be the interests of colonialism that will determine existence or non-existence of Israel.

Mr. Hashemi-Rafsanjani made the unprecedented threat as, following new suicide operations inside Israel and against Israeli settlements by Palestinian extremists in PA-controlled zones, responded by Israels heaviest bombarding of Palestinian cities, police, communication and radio-television installations, killing and wounding more than 200 people on both sides, resulted in the halting of all contacts between Israel and the PA of Mr. Yaser Arafat.

He said since Israel is the product of Western colonialism, the continued existence of Israel depends on interests of arrogance and colonialism and as long as the base is helpful for colonialism, it is going to keep it.

Hashemi-Rafsanjani advised Western states not to pin their hopes on Israels violence because it will be very dangerous.

We are not willing to see security in the world is harmed, he said, warning against the eruption of the Third World War.

War of the pious and martyrdom seeking forces against peaks of colonialism will be highly dangerous and might fan flames of the World War III, the former Iranian president said, backing firmly suicide operations against Israel.

Quoted by the official news agency IRNA, Mr. Hashemi-Rafsanjani said weakening of Palestinian Jihad is unlikely, as the Palestinians have come to the conclusion that talks would be effective only in light of struggle and self-sacrifice- the two key elements that gave way to beginning of the second Intifada

Iranian analysts and commentators outside Iran immediately reacted to Mr. Hashemi-Rafsanjanis statement, expressing fear that it might trigger an international backlash against Iran itself, giving Israel, the United States and other Western and even Arab nations to further isolate Iran as a source of threat to regional security.

Jews shall expect to be once again scattered and wandering around the globe the day when this appendix is extracted from the region and the

Muslim world, Mr. Hashemi-Rafsanjani warned, blaming on the United States and Britain the creation of the fabricated entity in the heart of Arab and Muslim world.

Chapter 10

Democracy in Iran

M any people in the West believe that the deadlock in Irans domestic politics blocks any hope for societal reform. But from my viewpoint here in Iran, there is hope. Let me tell you why.

Society itself, not the government, creates change. And there are deep transformations occurring in Iran. Out of sight of much of the world, Iran is inching its way toward democracy. The length of higher education in the country has been extended, absorbing the flow of job-seeking youths. This has hastened the transformation of thought and expectation in every corner of the country.

In military colleges, talk of human rights was, until very recently, totally unacceptable. Now courses on human rights have become part of the curriculum.

A 20 percent increase in the divorce rate is regrettable and worrisome, but it is also a sign that traditional marriage is changing as women gain equality. Other figures confirm this. Approximately 60 percent of university students are women, 12 percent of publishing house directors are women and 22 percent of the members of the Professional Association of Journalists are women.

In recent years some 8,000 nongovernmental organizations have been established throughout the country. These NGOs undercut the power of the state and fundamentalist ideas. Strengthening NGOs and civil institutions is one of the principal and most practical strategies to achieve social transformation.

In Baluchistan, one of the most deprived regions in the country, I was astonished to find several nongovernmental organizations led by women. These women are so confident in what they are doing that they challenge high officials and insist on their demands, a local official told me.

In a village 80 miles east of Tehran, the people have established their own local council. According to a prominent Iranian urban sociologist, In terms of its democratic structure this council could be regarded as exemplary. Every decision is made through democratic procedures; NGOs are created to support and inform the council on local affairs.

Not long ago traditional religion held that only believers were entitled to certain civil rights. Grand Ayatollah Hossein Ali Montazeri, one of the most prominent Shiite leaders, says that all people, regardless of their faith, are equally deserving of civil rights.

These are signs of a movement that will be impossible to stop. The state is facing powerful, irreversible social pressure for reform. If this movement is not responded to -- or, even worse, if it is repressed -- we would welcome another revolution. Weve learned from experience that a nonviolent, smooth domestic transformation would be far preferable to any change imposed from external sources.

Hope and courage are the main motives for change. I

remain hopeful and active in the Iranian movement to establish a democratic civil society.

The ***Student Movement Coordination Committee for Democracy in Iran*** (SMCCDI) is *completely independent of other groups and political affiliation as far as its administration and decision making is concerned.*

While a number of groups have often claimed the ownership of our organization and are trying to take credit in our name for our achievments, other have usurped or are currently using parts of our denomination in order to gain part of the trust that the name of the Student Movement Coordination Committee for Democracy in Iran is creating among many. Others have often published copies of our statements or articles under their names which have lead to confusion on our origin or goals.

Such behavior has harmed, at several occasions, the SMCCDI in many aspects and in its relations with third parties.

Its to note that the members of our Movement consist of students inside and outside of Iran, as well as Iranian professionals who share the students vision of a free, independent, democratic, secular and industrialized Iran. Although we have differing views for a post theocracy Iran, we are united based on our shared beliefs in nonviolent resistance, secularism, peace, democracy and free markets.

We believe the common objectives that unite those of us who oppose the theocracy are far greater than what divides us. Yet, we have allowed our differences to dictate our actions, permitting the theocracy to take advantage of our lack of unity. We need to come together and unite behind a set of principles and ideals, not an individual. No more individual worship. That time has long faded. How many times must we set up ourselves for disappointment by putting all of our hopes behind an individual?

We need to look forward to the future and create a better life for our children, not waste time placing blame for past mistakes or constantly criticizing one another. We need a tangible, constructive and positive action plan. Let us unite behind implementing peace, democracy, free markets and a bill of rights in Iran, while trusting the Iranian people to decide as to which government or individual suits them best.

We welcome any Iranian who believes in nonviolent resistance,

Hundreds of students of Khaje Nassir and of the Amir Kabir colleges of Tehran protested on 6th December 2006 against the persistent repression at the occasion of what has been, officially, named as the students day.

Students defied the massive presence of the Islamic regimes security forces and their check points in order to gather inside and outside the premises and broke the entry door in order to rally together.

Slogans, such as, Security feel shame and leave, Political prisoners must be free and Student will die but wont accept submission were shouted by students. Most students were seen taking their distances from the officially tolerated Office of Consolidation Unity (OCU), as they still remember of its founders role in the Islamic revolution, the US Hostages tragedy and their involvement in the sham theory of reforms from within the current regime. Such need of caution while needing to participate was underlined by SMCCDIs Coordinator in a TV interview program, broadcasted on Monday night, by the Los Angeles based Pars TV Network.

OCU had tried to seize the rally in its name.

Several students and some of their supporters were seen arrested by the security agents and put in special buses brought for the occasion.

Iranian people around the world and above all in Iran are demanding a free and secular democracy, human-rights and freedom. But since 25 years a tyrannical dictatorship in Iran ruling by a hand of non-elected criminal mullahs (known as so called reformers, conservatives or hardliners) - is suppressing brutally every efforts from the Iranian population for democracy and freedom.

It has attacked the vast majority of the Iranian population and consistently violated their rights with impunity. The main target of the assaults have shifted as the threat (or the perceived threat) to the regime has changed. Whether as principal, or lesser, opponents and dissenters the following groups have all been attacked throughout the reign of the mullahs, although with varying intensity.

1. Workers, trade unionists, left-wing and socialist activists;

2. Women and womens/feminist groups;

3. National and religious minorities;

4. Political oppositionists, including various monarchist, Islamic and liberal groups;

5. Writers, journalists, artists, intellectuals and students

6. Peasants and tribal groups;

7. Others who follow an un-Islamic life-style

8. The above groups cover the greater majority of the population of Iran and they have been under constant pressure and harassment, including hundreds of thousands arrests and tens of thousands of extra-

judicial executions. Tens of thousands are still in prison, including many who have completed their sentences.

Lets summarize some facts:

The Mullah-Dictatorship...

- is the terror-sponsor no. 1 (they support and work with terrorist groups worldwide).
- terrorizes the Iranian population and other human nation- and worldwide.
- has killed more than 200,000 Iranian-people since 1979.

Since 1979 the brutal dictatorship reign...

- the poverty (2/3 of the Iranian population live under the subsistence level),
- the crime,
- the bureaucratic inefficiency
- the illiteratism
- the lack of education and
- the environmental destruction
- have increased rapidly.

Further in marked contrast to the Iran till 1979 the women now have no rights and are separated from male in school, at work and at the publicly society...

- Every demonstration against the Terror-Regime will be beat up bloody ; death is the steady threat

for the demonstrators.
- Every criticism against the Mullah-Terrorism-Regime, whether in which way or wise, will be punished brutally:
  - jail,
  - stoning,
  - torture,
  - death through torture,
  - hanging,
  - bullwhips and

The people of Iran want freedom to move, to breathe, to laugh, to interact, to love, to hear music, to see color, to enjoy beauty, to experience life. They want freedom to live. Freedom begins when a man or woman enjoys rights, because he or she is an individual, a human being. This regime abhors freedom. This regime insists that by law all rights are its alone to give, and it confers what it pleases to give as privilege. This impulse to confine goes against the human grain and leads to tension and rage.

The people are aware of the destructive and deceitful nature of the Islamist regime. They fight in the universities, in the streets of our cities and in the alleys of our small towns. They want to be free and prosperous. Their choice is not between one or the other faction of the regime. Rather, it is between a theocracy that constitutionally denies them their rights and a secular government that will respect their rights and freedoms as a sovereign people. They know that unless the state is liberated from the tyranny of the clerical establishment they can be neither free nor prosperous. Already, Iranians have begun to use the language of liberation a language beyond the discourse of the Islamic Republic.

Chapter 11

A.Q. Khan Network
A Walmart for WMD

Pakistans nuclear weapons program is a source of extreme national pride, and, as its father, A.Q. Khan -- who headed Pakistans nuclear program for some 25 years -- is considered a national hero. Though his full name is Abdul Qadeer Khan, he is commonly referred to as A.Q. Khan. Born in Bhopal, Dr. A.Q. Khan is a German-educated metallurgist who, from May 1972 to December1975 was employed by Physics Dynamic Research Laboratory (also known as FDO), an engineering firm based in Amsterdam and a subcontractor to the URENCO consortium specializing in the manufacture of nuclear equipment. A Dutch-German and British consortium, Urenco primary enrichment facility was at Almelo, Netherlands. A.Q. Khan, in his capacity would eventualy have an office at that facility by late 1974.

In 1975, following Indias 1974 nuclear test and while on holiday in Pakistan, Dr. was reported to have been asked by the then-prime minister to take charge of Pakistans uranium-enrichment program. In early 1976, Dr. Khan left the Netherlands with secret URENCO blueprints for uranium centrifuge (one of Dutch origins featuring an aluminum rotor, and another of German make, composed of maraging steel, a superhard alloy). Convicted in 1983 in abstentia by a court in the Netherlands for stealing the designs, his conviction would be later overturned on a technicality.

Because Pakistan lacked the technical base to for a nuclear program, Khan reportedly began to clandestinely acquire the necessary materials and components required for the production of fissile material using information pertaining to URENCOs key suppliers, which he had also taken with him from the Netherlands. Theses were used to provide Pakistan with needed equipment. Indeed, according to a Dutch government report, two Dutch firms were involved in the 1976 export of 6,200 unfinished maraging steel rotor tubes to Pakistan. A dual track approach was reportedly used for Pakistans nuclear weapons program, however, with Khans program being the reportedly inferior one, as far as size, power and efficiency characteristics were concerned. Pakistans Atomic Energy Commission ran the other track. There have however been a number of allegations regarding Pakistans nuclear weapon that its origins may lie with China, as Pakistans bombs closely mirror Chinese designs from the late 1960s, and which relied on advanced, implosion-based detonation.

A.Q. Khan initially worked under Pakistan Atomic Energy Commission (PAEC), headed by Munir Ahmad Khan, for a short period. But the pair fell out, and in July 1976, Bhutto gave A.Q. Khan autonomous control of the uranium enrichment project, reporting directly to the prime ministers office, which arrangement has continued since. A.Q. Khan founded the Engineering Research Laboratories (ERL) on 31 July 1976, with the exclusive task of indigenous development of Uranium Enrichment Plant. Within the next five years the target would be achieved. On 01 May 1981, ERL was renamed by Gen. Mohammad Zia ul-Haq as Dr. A.Q. Khan Research Laboratories (KRL). It was enrichment of Uranium in KRL that ultimately led to the successful detonation of Pakistans first nuclear device on 28 May 1998.

During the 1990s, there were intermittent clues from intelligence that AQ Khan was discussing the sale of nuclear technology to countries of concern. By early 2000, intelligence revealed that these were not isolated incidents. It became clear that Khan was at the centre of an international proliferation network. By April 2000, the UK Joint Intelligence Committee (JIC) was noting that there was an evolving, and as yet incomplete, picture of the supply of uranium enrichment equipment to at least one customer in the Middle East, thought to be Libya, and evidence linking this activity to Khan.

A.Q. Khans official career came to an abrupt end in March 2001, when he was suddenly was forced out as director of the nuclear lab by order of President Pervez Musharraf. Though Kahn was made a special adviser to the government, the reason for his dismissal reportedly coincided with concerns about financial improprieties at the lab as well as general warnings from the United States to the Musharraf about Khans proliferation activities. Musharrafs restraint in dealing with A.Q. Khan has been said to have resulted from the lack of incontrovertible evidence of proliferation activities. Nonetheless, Deputy Secretary of State Richard Armitage, in an article which appeared in the Financial Times on 01 June 2001, expressed concern that, people who were employed by the nuclear agency and have retired may be assisting North Korea with its nuclear program.

The change in position for A.Q. Khan did not necessarily end proliferation concerns. Indeed, while in Pakistan in October 2003, a US delegation led by Deputy Secretary of State Richard L. Armitage reportedly briefed Gen. Musharraf on A.Q. Khan activities. Gen. Abizaid, then head of US Central Command, repotedly conducted similar concerns to Pakistani political and military leaders.

With the international inspections of Irans nuclear operations and the October 2003 interception of a ship headed for Libya and carrying centrifuge parts, Pakistan began seriously investigating A.Q. Khan. The United Nations International Atomic Energy Agency in November 2003 itself warned Pakistan of possible nuclear leaks. After two months of investigations, in late January 2004 Pakistani officials concluded that two of the countrys most senior nuclear scientists had black market contacts that supplied sensitive technology to Iran and Libya. Pakistani intelligence officials said the scientists - A.Q. Khan and Mohammed Farooq - provided the help both directly and through a black market based in the Persian Gulf emirate of Dubai. Dr. Khan and Dr. Farooq were longtime colleagues at A.Q. Khan Research Laboratories. President Musharraf acknowledged that some scientists may have acted for their own personal gain, but he denied any government involvement and pledged harsh punishment for any person implicated in the scandal.

The lack of of strict oversight over Pakistans nuclear weapons program has been blamed with a brigadier general in charge of security for Dr. Khans top-secret laboratory never having reported anything. Doubts remain, however, about the lack of governmental approval/supervision of A.Q. Kahns proliferation activities; some of which were conspicuously advertised. Indeed, one of A.Q. Khan Research Laboratories sales brochure promoted the sale of components derived from Pakistans nuclear weapons program and critical to the making of centrifuges. The Pakistani government istelf published in 2000 an advertisement regarding procedures to be followed for the exports of nuclear material according to a Congressional Research Service report dated May 2003. Moreover, Khan and colleagues of his had published numerous scientific papers internationally on the making and testing of uranium centrifuges, including one dated from 1991 which detailed the methodology to be followed in ecthing grooves on the bottom of a centrifuge to aid the flow of lubricants and thus aid in the centrifuges spinning speed.

Some questions have been raised over the idea that even someone as prominent as Khan could have delivered such sensitive material without approval from higher authorities, and that at the very least the leadership of Pakistans military and intelligence establishment must have sanctioned the transfers. The extent of previous Pakistani civilian governments involvement is unclear, even if the military knew and approved the transfers. This is partly a result of the distrust by the army of civilian politicians. Such was the case with former Prime Ministers Benazir Bhutto and Nawaz Sharif.

Many Pakistanis have felt that President Pervez Musharraf succumbed to US pressure in moving against A.Q. Khan, the latters stature as a national hero. However, given the scope of the problem and the fact taht the three intended recipients of nuclear transfers are on the list of countries the United States is most anxious to keep away from weapons of mass destruction, Musharraf may not have had a choice other than act on A.Q. Khan. Still, the government of Pakistan is likely not to be eager to give the United States any more information than it has to as to the whereabouts and/or security arrangements of its nuclear arsenal.

In his startling televised confession Wednesday, Abdul Qadeer Khan insisted he acted without authorization in selling nuclear technology to other governments. A.Q. Khan admitted selling nuclear technology to Iran, Libya, and North Korea. A.Q. Khan asked for clemency, but the Pakistani government made no public announcement about whether he is to be prosecuted. The confessed proliferation took place between 1989 and 2000, though it is suspected that proliferation activities to North Korea continued after that date. The network used to supply these activities is global in scope, stretching from Germany to Dubai and from China to South Asia, and involves numerous middlemen and suppliers.

A.Q. Khan & Iran

Khans proliferation activities help explain the close resemblance born by Irans nuclear centrifuge technology to that of Pakistan. In 1987 Iranian revolutionary guard members met with representative of A.Q. Khans network Dubai to purchase 500 Centrifuges to make highly enriched Uranium needed for Nuclear Weapons. They also acquired some weapons designs as well.

Following Irans disclosure of uranium enrichment research and subsequent inspections, the central role of Pakistan in Irans nuclear programme was unearthed. This was compounded by Iran turning over to the IAEA a complete history of its nuclear program including a listing of middlemen and scientists linked to Pakistan and A.Q. Khan.

Evidence uncovered by inspectors showed that Pakistan and Iran agreed around 1987 to a deal whereby a Pakistani centrifuge design was provided to Iran to resolve the latters previous unsuccessful attempts to master uranium enrichment technology. The transfer of nuclear technology began in 1989, though Khan is said to have claimed to have discontinued the sale two years later. The IAEA, though, reportedly has evidence that Pakistani assistance continued as late as 1996. At that time, the countries differing policies in dealing with the Taliban regime in Afghanistan soured their relations, though it has been claimed the Pakistani assistance continued nonetheless.

According to confessions by A.Q. Khan and aides of his to Pakistani investigators reportedly implicated among others, Gen. Mirza Aslam Beg, the commander of Pakistans army from 1988-1991, and that any nuclear technology shared with Iran had been approved by him. These charges were denied by him. Pakistan did discover evidence that Beg had been informed by Khan of the transfer to Iran in early 1991 of outdated hardware, though it has been claimed that A.Q. Khan had led him to believe that the material would not allow Iran to produce enriched uranium. Conflicting this assertion is Khan who is said to have admitted that Gen. Beg had approved the technology transfer.

A.Q. Khan has claimed that equipment and drawing shipped to Iran were supplied as a result of pressure from the late Gen. Imtiaz during his tenure as defense advisor to Prime Minister Benazir Bhutto from December 1988 to August 1990 . Khan has also admitted to meeting Iranian scientists in Karachi at the request of Dr. Niazi, a close Bhutto aide. In return for the help, Iran transferred millions of dollars to foreign bank accounts, with some money funnelled through the Bank of Credit and Commerce International. That bank collapsed in 1991.

Some of the centrifuges examined also appeared to have been used outside Iran to enrich uranium, while components of some centrifuges appeared to have come directly from Pakistan. Though some of the machines Iran had bought did not work properly, Iran reportedly still managed to effect significant improvements on Pakistani equipment designs. Despite the design similarities, Iran has nonetheless denied having received them from Pakistan.

Faced with disclosure, Khan reportedly contacted Iranian officials to not only urge them to destroy some of their facilities but also to pretend that the Pakistanis who had assisted them had died.

In early March 2005, Pakistan acknowledged A. Q. Khan had provided centrifuges to Iran, though it denied having had any knowledge of the transactions.

Iran and South Africa

Even with the help of A.Q Khan networks help Iran was still searching for technical help and parts to build a nuclear weapon, they found it in Johannesburg, South Africa where apartheid wound down and the government were looking to dismantle their own arsenal of nuclear weapons. Perfect place for Iran to go shopping for advance weapons technology which could eventually have nuclear capabilities.

The Iranian agents who were sent to Johannesburg were intercepted arrested and sent back to Iran by the CIA and Mossad agents as part of a counterterrorism operation known as Operation Shock Wave. The idea was to send a shockwave through the intelligence network of Iran that any attempt to seek nuclear weapons technology would be met with the same fate and that they are being watched.

A.Q. Khan & Libya

By April 2000, the UK Joint Intelligence Committee (JIC) was noting that there was an evolving, and as yet incomplete, picture of the supply of uranium enrichment equipment to at least one customer in the Middle East, thought to be Libya, and evidence linking this activity to Khan. By September 2000, it was pointing out that the network was expanding to mass-produce components for large-scale centrifuge cascades. During 2001,the JIC continued to track AQ Khan s activities. An assessment by the UK in March 2002 pulled together all the strands of intelligence on AQ Khan then available. The conclusions showed the wide spread of Khans network and that he had moved his base outside Pakistan and was now controlling it through his associates in Dubai. At the same time, intelligence showed that he had now established his own production facilities, in Malaysia. He was being helped in his activities by a network of associates and suppliers, including BSA Tahir (a Sri Lankan businessman operating out of Dubai). By July 2002,the JIC had concluded that AQ Khan s network was central to all aspects of the Libyan nuclear weapons program.

Evidence uncovered as part of Libyas decision to come clean on its weapons of mass destruction programs show further implication on the part of A.Q. Khan and, possibly, Pakistan. Indeed, Libyas uranium enrichment program appeared reliant on both G-1 and G-2 (P-1 and P-2) centrifuge designs; material for which it reportedly paid substantial sums for.

Started in the early 1990s, Libyas disclosed uranium enrichment program appears based on both Pakistans G-1 and G-2 centrifuge designs, with some of the centrifuges having been flown there from Pakistan.

A.Q. Khan has confessed to meeting with Libyans in Istanbul, Turkey, in 1990.

Libya was also reportedly provided by the Pakistanis with additional information on how and where to acquire additional components for this program. Using at first the G-1 design, it later upgraded to the G-2 model, which Libya is reported to have had set up a small number of. These were being manufactured at a facility in Malaysia arranged through Khans network. Components from that plant which were intercepted by the United States aboard a German-registered ship on their way to Libya in October 2003 after having been spotted whilst going through the Suez Canal.

Schematics for both G-2 centrifuges and bombs were reported to be among documentation given to both the United States and the IAEA by Libya.

The supply chain for Libyas program relied on Libyans contacting Pakistanis who would in turn contact middleman. These would contact suppliers for the desired components which, once completed would then be shipped to the Persian Gulf emirate of Dubai, from where they would be delivered to Libya. Items thus procured ranges from high-strength metals and vacuum systems to electronics.

A.Q. Khan and North Korea

A.Q. Khans network is reported to have played a significant role in North Koreas nuclear program, providing it with an alternative way of manufacturing nuclear fuel, after it agreed under the 1994 Agreed Framework to freeze its reactors and reprocessing facilities. In all, A.Q. Khans network provided North Korea with both centrifuge designs and a small number of actual, complete centrifuges, in addition to a list of components needed to manufacture additional ones.

It is also in 1994 that then Pakistani Prime Minister Benazir Bhutto traveled to North Korea reportedly at the request of the then-army chief of staff, Gen. Abudl Waheed. Buttho claimed that Pakistan paid for North Korean assistance, returning, at Khans insistence and desire for nuclear-capable long range missiles, from a trip to Pyongyang with computer disks containing specifications for missiles. Somome sources are, however, reportedly claimed that lack of money on Pakistans part made trading easier.

A few months later, A.Q. Khan made the first of what would be about 13 trips to North Korea, as part of a Pakistani delegation to Pyongyang, composed of both scientists and military officers. At that time Musharraf was Waheeds director general for military operations. While there, he is said to have helped N. Korea with the design and equipping of facilities focused on the enrichment of uranium in exchange for North Korean assistance in the area of missile technology. Khan confessed to helping North Korea with the knowledge and approval of senior military commanders, among which two army chiefs and Musharraff. Waheed was subsequently replaced in January 1996 by Gen. Karamat who secretely travelled to North Korea in December 1997.

Khan has claimed that Karamat was also aware of the terms of the barter deal between N. Korea and Pakistan, since Pakistan successfully test-fired a Ghauri missile in April 1998. Implicit are claims that Musharraf must have been aware of the Pakistani-North Korean agreement given that after becoming army chief of staff in October 1998, Musharraf also took over the Ghauri program.

In exchanged, North Korea is ordered for the delivery of P-1 centrifuge components between 1997-1999, with A.Q. Khans network providing direct technical assistance between the years 1998-2000.

In 2000, Pakistans Inter-Services Intelligence conducted a raid on an aircraft chartered by the Khan Lab and bound for North Korea. Up until then, it has been claimed, senior military commanders had been unaware of Khans dealings with North Korea. The raid yielded no evidence, however, but Khan was reported to have been warned against engaging in proliferating activities. As late as July 2002, Pakistani cargo planes were spotted by US Spy satellites in Pyongyang being loaded with missile parts. Musharraf claimed that these were picking up surface-to-air missiles Pakistan had purchased. One account has that Kahn not only transferred P-1 and P-2 centrifuges to North Korea, but also drawing, sketches and technical data as well as depleted uranium hexafluoride gas.

In April 2003, a cargo-ship containing a aluminum tubing was intercepted in the Suez Canal following German conclusion that it was headed for North Korea. The specifications of the tubes suggested that they were intended for use as outer casings for G-2(P-2) centrifuges, which A. Q. Khan had written about.

Following additional questionning, it has been reported that A.Q. Khan admitted to, during a 1999 visit to an undisclosed location about one hour our of Pyongyang, witnessing first hand what were described to be three plutonium nuclear devices produced by North Korea.

In mid-to-late August 2005, Pakistani President Pervez Musharraf for the first time confirmed, during an interview with the Japanese news agency Kyodo, that Abdul Qadeer Khan had transferred both centrifuges and centrifuge parts as well as their designs on to North Korea.

The most disturbing aspect of the international nuclear smuggling network headed by Abdul Qadeer Khan, is how poorly the nuclear nonproliferation regime fared in exposing and stopping the networks operation. Khan, with the help of associates on four continents, managed to buy and sell key nuclear weapons capabilities for more than two decades while eluding the worlds best intelligence agencies and nonproliferation institutions and organizations. Despite a wide range of hints and leads, the United States and its allies failed to thwart this network throughout the 1980s and 1990s as it sold the equipment and expertise needed to produce nuclear weapons to major U.S. enemies including Iran, Libya, and North Korea.

By 2000, U.S. intelligence had at least partially penetrated the networks operations, leading to many revelations and ultimately, in October 2003, the dramatic seizure of uranium-enrichment gas-centrifuge components bound for Libyas secret nuclear weapons program aboard the German-owned ship BBC China. Libyas subsequent renunciation of nuclear weapons led to further discoveries about the networks operations and the arrest of many of its key players, including Khan himself.

The Khan network has caused enormous damage to efforts aimed at stopping the spread of nuclear weapons, to U.S. national security, and to international peace and stability. Without assistance from the network, it is unlikely that Iran would have been able to develop the ability to enrich uranium using gas centrifuges—now that countrys most advanced and threatening nuclear program. Suspicions also remain that members of the network may have helped Al Qaeda obtain nuclear secrets prior to the fall of the Taliban regime in Afghanistan. The damage caused by this network led former CIA director George Tenet to reportedly describe Khan as being at least as dangerous as Osama bin Laden. The Khan network succeeded for many years by exploiting weaknesses in export control systems and recruiting suppliers, including some in states that were members of the Nuclear Suppliers Group (NSG). The networks key customers were states contemptuous of NSG controls and committed to violating the Nuclear Non-Proliferation Treaty (NPT) in their quest for secret nuclear capabilities. In essence, the network adapted to and benefited from the discriminatory and voluntary export control regime that was embodied in the NSG and complementary national export control systems. There is little confidence that other networks do not or will not exist or that elements of the Khan network will not reconstitute themselves in the future.

Yet, the international response thus far has not been sufficiently effective. Although revelations about the Khan network have reenergized support for a range of reforms, more extensive improvements to the international nonproliferation regime are still needed to block the emergence of new networks and to detect them promptly if they do arise. The United States, with the help of its allies, needs to pursue a broad range of foreign policy, intelligence, nonproliferation, export control, and law enforcement initiatives, as well as policies designed to close down nuclear smugglers access to civilian industries in newly emerging industrial states.

Pakistan, Khan, and the Nuclear Black Market. Revelations in February 2004 that Pakistans premier nuclear scientist, Dr. A.Q. Khan, was behind an illicit nuclear trafficking network raised international concern about the threat posed by the proliferation of nuclear know-how and equipment.

Khan confessed to Pakistani security officials that he had transferred nuclear-related technologies to Iran, Libya, and North Korea, but denied that he received any support from the Pakistani government. President Musharraf pardoned Khan following Khans public confession aired on national television, but placed the scientist under house arrest pending a more thorough investigation by the Inter Services Intelligence (ISI). The official position of the Bush administration is that Pakistans government did not know about or support Khans activities. However, many analysts believe that given Khans connections to the Pakistani leaders and the military and the size of his black market operation, Pakistans government must have been aware of his illicit activities. Pakistan has refused to let foreign officials question Khan, although it cooperated with the International Atomic Energy Agencys investigation into the origin of enriched uranium particles found in nuclear facilities in Iran.

In May 2006, Pakistans government declared closed its investigation into the Khan nuclear proliferation network. Khan remains under house arrest. Around the world, most participants in the network have not been charged or punished for helping to provide nuclear weapons technology to Iran, Libya, North Korea, and other countries, and smuggling of such technology continues.

Client States and Middlemen.

Several middlemen in countries around the world played a significant role in helping Khan deliver illicit goods to client states. Buhary Syed Abu Tahir, a middleman in Malaysia, helped Khan deliver centrifuge parts and blueprints to Iran and Libya. Tahir subsequently identified middlemen that operated out of Germany, Turkey, Switzerland, and the United Kingdom. Khans network also supplied North Korea with centrifuge technology and depleted uranium hexaflouride gas between 1997 and 2002. Khan is believed to have personally visited Pyongyang 12 times during this time period.

The Aftermath: New Pakistani Export Control Law.

The Khan network has revealed how weak Pakistans pre-existing export control laws were. Pakistan had passed export legislation in July 1998, February 1999, August 1999, and again in November 2000. Several loopholes and contradictions permeated these laws, and, facing increased international pressure in light of the Khan revelations, Pakistan moved to pass a new export control bill on July 7, 2004. The legislation, known as the Export Control on Goods, Technologies, Material, and Equipment Related to Nuclear and Biological Weapons and their Delivery Systems Act, was ratified by the Pakistan National Assembly and the Senate on September 19, 2004. The bill entails harsh penalties for violators, including up to 14 years imprisonment, seizure of personal assets, and a fine of up to 5 million rupees ($86,500 dollars).

After years of blanket denials, Pakistans government has finally admitted that during 1989-2003 Pakistani nuclear scientists and entities proliferated nuclear weapons-related technologies, equipment, and know how to Iran, North Korea, and Libya. The Pakistani governments denials collapsed after Libya formally decided to terminate its clandestine weapons of mass destruction (WMD) programs in October 2003 and make a full disclosure of its efforts to build nuclear weapons; and after Iran, in fall 2003, agreed to cooperate with the International Atomic Energy Agency (IAEA) and provide details of its clandestine uranium enrichment programs that originated in the mid-1980s.

The Iranian and Libyan revelations have exposed a vast black market in clandestine nuclear trade comprising of middle men and shell companies; clandestine procurement techniques; false end-user certifications; transfer of blueprints from one country, manufacture in another, transshipment to a third, before delivery to its final destination. But even more remarkably, the investigations of Iranian and Libyan centrifuge-based uranium enrichment efforts have exposed the central role of the former head of Pakistans Khan Research Laboratories (KRL), Dr. A.Q. Khan, in the clandestine trade. Detailed information has surfaced about transfers of technical drawings, design specifications, components, complete assemblies of Pakistans P-1 and P-2 centrifuge models, including the blueprint of an actual nuclear warhead from KRL. But the transfer of hardware apart, there is equally damning evidence that Khan and his top associates imparted sensitive knowledge and know how in secret technical briefings for Iranian, North Korean, and Libyan scientists in Pakistan and other locations abroad.

Three decades ago, Khan, with the support of Pakistans government, set out to create a new model of proliferation. He used centrifuge design blueprints and supplier lists of companies that he had pilfered from URENCOs facility in the Netherlands to launch Pakistans nuclear weapons program. In the process, he perfected a clandestine model of trade in forbidden technologies outside formal government controls. By the end of the 1980s, after KRL acquired the wherewithal to produce highly-enriched uranium for a nuclear weapons program, it reversed course and began vending its services to other clients in the international system. KRL and Khans first client was Iran (or possibly China even earlier); but the list gradually expanded to include North Korea and Libya. Starting in the late 1980s, Khan and some of his top associates began offering a one-stop shop for countries that wished to acquire nuclear technologies for a weapons program. Khans key innovation was to integrate what was earlier a disaggregated market place for such technologies, design, engineering, and consultancy services; and in the process offer clients the option of telescoping the time required to develop a nuclear weapons capability.

As independent evidence of diversions from KRL has come to light, the Pakistani government has swiftly sought to distance itself from Khan and his activities. President Pervez Musharrafs regime has publicly denied that it or past Pakistani state authorities ever authorized transfers or sales of sensitive nuclear weapons-related technologies to Iran, Libya, or North Korea. Islamabad attributes Khans clandestine nuclear trade to personal financial corruption, abuse of authority, and megalomania. Alarmed that Khans past indiscretions might directly implicate the Pakistani military and state authorities, the Musharraf regime also launched an internal probe to apparently get a clearer picture of the activities of its top nuclear lab and senior scientists. In fall 2003, Pakistani investigators traveled to Iran, Dubai, Vienna, and Libya to investigate US and IAEA complaints against Khan. They discovered that the complaints were borne out by evidence; and more alarmingly, that Khan had apparently made unauthorized deals unbeknownst to Islamabad and reaped huge personal financial rewards in the process.

Since October-November 2003, Khan and his close associates movements have been restricted. While Khan himself has been under placed under informal house arrest, his aides are undergoing what Pakistani government spokesmen politely describe as debriefing sessions. In late January 2004, the government ultimately stripped Khan of his cabinet rank and fired him from his position as senior advisor to the chief executive. As part of a deal, Khan made a public apology on television before the Pakistani nation. In that apology, he admitted to personal failings, accepted responsibility for all past proliferation activities, and absolved past and present Pakistani state authorities of any complicity in his acts. In return, the Jamali cabinet granted Khan a conditional pardon. However, Khans senior aides remain in custody and the government has not made up its mind on whether to press formal charges against them for violating the states national secrets or to pardon them.

Most proliferation specialists and independent observers of Pakistani politics have watched the surreal saga of what is perhaps the greatest proliferation scandal in history with disbelief.

Most also find the Pakistani governments assertions of innocence and attempts to absolve itself of any responsibility in the matter astonishing. For most, the mammoth scale of the diversion from KRL, its extended time span, the logistics of transporting material and machines out of Pakistan, and the difficulty of circumventing the security detail surrounding senior Pakistani scientists and KRL, are obvious pointers to state complicity. In the past three months, senior Pakistani politicians have raked up the historical record to point fingers at the Pakistani Army. Others, including US government officials, have alluded to indicators that at least some of Khans activities might have enjoyed tacit, if not formal sanction from oversight authorities within the state. Such indicators include Islamabads past unresponsiveness to diplomatic entreaties, sharing of intelligence inputs, published documentary records, informed public speculation about Khan and KRLs nuclear proliferation activities, and the Pakistani militarys corporate ability to sustain its WMD programs on a weak military-industrial base, even as the state operated at the margins of economic solvency. As new evidence surfaces by the day, the record becomes clearer; even as the controversy surrounding the role of the past and present Pakistani governments becomes uglier.

This research report provides an overview of the evidence that has surfaced in the last three months to paint a clearer picture of what we now know of Khan and KRLs contributions to Iran, North Korea, and Libyas clandestine centrifuge-based uranium enrichment programs. It reviews the internal debate and finger pointing in Pakistan, and analyzes the narrative presented by President Musharrafs regime in its defense. The report also outlines some of the reasons for the Bush administrations muted response and concludes by offering a net assessment of the strategic implications of the new disclosures.

What Do We Now Know?

Although Pakistan has admitted that its nuclear scientists and entities engaged in clandestine nuclear transfers to Iran, North Korea, and Libya during the period 1989-2003, the full extent and nature of those transfers are still unclear. Iran has still not made a full disclosure about its two-decades-old centrifuge enrichment program. Scientists and engineers at the US Department of Energy are still in the process of analyzing documents and equipment turned over by Libya. And North Korea maintains that it never admitted to pursuing a clandestine centrifuge-based uranium enrichment program in October 2002.

But despite existing gaps, there is evidence that nuclear transfers to Iran from Pakistan occurred during 1989-1995. According to Pakistani government sources, North Korea obtained similar assistance between the years 1997-2001. However, US intelligence agencies believe that strategic trade between Pyongyang and Islamabad continued as late as August 2002. Khan also began cooperating with Libya in 1997and such cooperation continued until fall 2003.

All three countries - Iran, North Korea, and Libya - obtained blueprints, technical design data, specifications, components, machinery, enrichment equipment, models, and notes related to KRLs first generation P-1 and the next generation P-2 centrifuges.

Cooperation between Pakistan and Iran most likely began in 1987 after the two countries signed a secret agreement on nuclear cooperation for peaceful purposes. Apparently, Khan sold disused P-1 centrifuges and what he describes as outmoded equipment to Iran along with the drawings and technical specifications and possibly components or complete assemblies of the more advanced P-2 model. Initial deliveries were made during the years 1989-1991; but evidence has surfaced that transfers continued as late as 1995. Pakistani investigators believe that some of the shipments were probably transported over land through a Karachi-based businessman. Other shipments were routed through Dubai.

Similarly, Khan and his associates supplied Pyongyang with centrifuge and enrichment machines, and depleted uranium hexaflouride gas (UF6). Orders for the North Korean contract were placed in 1997 and deliveries continued until 1999. KRL also rendered further technical assistance to Pyongyang during 1999-2001. Some of the shipments to North Korea were flown directly from Pakistan using chartered and Pakistan Air Force transports.

In 1997 Khan supplied Libya with 20 assembled P-1 centrifuges; with components for an additional 200 more for a pilot facility. The Libyans also obtained 1.87-tons of UF6 in 2001; the consignment was directly airlifted from Pakistan on board a Pakistani airline. IAEA sources believe that amount is consistent with the requirements for a pilot enrichment facility. In September 2000, Libya placed an order for 10,000 centrifuges of the more advanced P-2 model. Component parts for the centrifuges began arriving in Libya by December 2002. However, a subsequent consignment of parts was intercepted by US intelligence agencies in October 2003, after which Libya decided to make a full disclosure and terminate its nuclear weapons program. But more alarmingly, in either late 2001 or early 2002, Khan also transferred the blueprint of an actual fission weapon to Libya as an added bonus.

The supply package to all the three countries did not just include hardware and design information. Khan and his associates also provided their clients integrated shopping solutions in a fragmented market. They shared sensitive information on supplier networks, manufacturers, clandestine procurement and smuggling techniques, and arranged for the manufacture, transport, and delivery of equipment and materials through a clutch of companies and middlemen based in South-East Asia, the Middle East, Africa, and Europe. Pakistani scientists and technicians held multiple briefing sessions for their Iranian counterparts in Karachi, and locations in Malaysia and Iran. Briefings for Libyan scientists were held in Casablanca and Istanbul. Khan also visited North Korea nearly a dozen times, and it is likely that technical briefing sessions for North Korean scientists were arranged during those visits. But there are also reports that North Korean scientists were allowed to train at KRL itself. In addition, Pakistani engineers and scientists were also on hand for providing consulting advice and trouble-shooting services through intermediaries.

US intelligence analysts believe that the nuclear weapon blueprint that Khan and his network sold Libya is most likely a design that China tested in the late 1960s; and later shared with Pakistan. Apparently the design documents transferred from Pakistan contain information in both Chinese and English, establishing their Chinese lineage; they also provide conclusive evidence of past Chinese assistance to Pakistans nuclear weapons program. The blueprint provides the design parameters and engineering specifications on how to build an implosion weapon weighing over 1,000 pounds that could be delivered using aircraft or a large ballistic missile. Analysts believe that the design is not currently in use in Pakistan, which has graduated to building more advanced nuclear weapons. However, the transfer of an actual weapon design to Tripoli has left open the question whether Tehran and Pyongyang obtained a similar copy; whether the design is still in circulation; or who else might have obtained it.

In the mid-1990s, Khan also set up a clandestine meeting with a top Syrian official in Beirut to offer help with setting up a centrifuge enrichment facility for an HEU-based nuclear weapons program. In mid-1990, he also made a similar offer through a Gulf-based intermediary to Saddam Husseins regime. However, the Iraqi government ignored the offer in the erroneous belief that it was likely a sting operation or a scam. There is also fragmentary and indirect evidence to suggest that Khan may have offered his nuclear services to Saudi Arabia and the United Arab Emirates.

But little is publicly know about the outcome of those overtures.

The Internal Blame Game

The Pakistani government claims that the nuclear trade with Iran, North Korea, and Libya was unauthorized; that KRL proliferated centrifuge technologies, equipment, and related intellectual property clandestinely and illegally, unbeknownst to military oversight authorities formally in charge of the nuclear weapons program. Pakistani President Pervez Musharraf has publicly accused A.Q. Khan and his top aides of corruption and attributed their actions to financial gains.

In an attempt to distance Pakistani state authorities from the scandals fallout, Musharraf has also suggested that the scientists were rogue operators, who abused the trust and autonomy granted by state authorities to pursue their personal agendas.

In calculated leaks to the press, senior Pakistani government officials have painted Khan as a megalomaniac; a publicity hound who created a larger-than-life image of himself. They have narrated tales of KRLs corrupt culture; of Khans parceling of procurement contracts at exorbitant prices to family members and associates; bribes for procurement orders from vendors; Khans palatial houses and real estate investments in Pakistan and abroad; his lavish lifestyle; and unaccounted for millions in secret bank accounts.

Pakistani government sources from the president on down have also made it plain that Khans corruption and profiteering from proliferation activities were critical factors behind his removal from KRL in March 2001.

However, Khan has disputed Musharrafs allegations in private debriefings with Pakistani government investigators. Apparently Khan has made the case that he was pressured to sell nuclear technologies to Iran by two individuals close to former Prime Minister Benazir Bhutto. The first, Dr. Niazi, was a friend, while the latter, General Imtiaz Ali, served as military advisor to Bhutto.

Both individuals are now deceased. Khan has further alleged that aid for Irans uranium enrichment program was also approved by then Chief of Army Staff, General (ret.) Mirza Aslam Beg (1988-1991). Similarly, Khan claims the nuclear-for-missile deal with the Kim Jong Il regime was backed by two former army chiefs, Generals (ret.) Abdul Waheed Kakar (1993-1996) and Jehangir Karamat (1996-1998). The latter, according to Khan, made a secret trip to North Korea in December 1997 and presided over efforts to obtain Nodong ballistic missiles from that country. Khans friends have also privately suggested that General Pervez Musharraf, who succeeded Karamat and took over responsibility for the Ghauri missile program in 1998, had to have known about the transfers to North Korea.

In interviews with Pakistani government investigators, Khan apparently insisted that no investigation would be complete until all the actors - Khan, former army chiefs, and other senior military and government officials - were questioned together. Equally significant, Khan is believed to have challenged his interlocutors reticence to probe the *nature* of the technology and equipment transfers to North Korea as against the blanket charge of proliferation; the import of his suggestion being that either the equipment and material transferred to North Korea would not enable it to enrich uranium to weapons-grade in the short-term, or alternatively, that the logistics of the equipment and technology transfers would directly implicate the military and state authorities. There are also rumors that Khan has smuggled out evidence with his daughter Dina, who is a British citizen, which would directly implicate senior Pakistani officials in an unfolding scandal.

Fearing that any further washing of Pakistans dirty nuclear laundry in public could cause irretrievable harm to the Pakistani military and state authorities, Musharraf has sought to cap the controversy by pardoning Khan for his past transgressions. In the bargain, Khan has accepted personal responsibility for all acts of proliferation and absolved the Pakistani state and the military from blame. However, in his contrite public confession on television, Khan declared that he acted in good faith but on errors of judgment, obliquely hinting at the likely involvement of the Pakistani military and other state authorities in his activities.

Despite the Pakistani governments attempts to absolve itself from the charges of proliferation, most independent analysts of Pakistani politics remain unconvinced that A.Q. Khan and his associates could have engaged in nuclear transfers over nearly two decades without sanction or tacit acknowledgement from sections or individuals within the Pakistani government. The Pakistani militarys tight control over the nuclear weapons program, multiple layers of security surrounding it, the exports of machinery and hardware from Pakistan, as well as rumors, leaks, and past warnings about Pakistans nuclear cooperation with Iran and North Korea by Western intelligence agencies, have led analysts to believe that the current effort to pin the blame on a small number of senior officials from KRL is a cynical ploy to prevent the Pakistani military and state from being implicated in the unfolding scandal.

Musharrafs Narrative

Pakistani President Pervez Musharraf has deployed four arguments to explain why Khan and his associates were able to proliferate nuclear technologies and secrets for nearly two decades without the knowledge of successive Pakistani governments.

First, he has argued that during the covert phase of Pakistans nuclear weapons program, which lasted from 1975-1998, A.Q. Khan and KRL had to rely on shell companies, clandestine procurement techniques, smuggling networks, and middlemen for the purchase of equipment and technologies that were on the export control lists of advanced industrial countries. Thus the same networks that supplied the Pakistani nuclear weapons effort were redirected to meet the demand for similar technologies in the international market. Once Khan and his associates developed a successful model of clandestine trade in forbidden technologies outside formal governmental control, they were able to offer their services for financial rewards to other bidders in the international system.

During a press briefing earlier in February, Musharraf explained that since Pakistans nuclear weapons program was covert until 1998, civilian governments were out of the nuclear decision-making loop. But more astonishingly, he sought to peddle the line that even former army chiefs, who were supposed to exercise oversight authority over KRL, never knew of the intimate happenings within the entity. Musharrafs proffered explanation for successive army chiefs ignorance: the KRLs near total organizational autonomy. According to Musharraf, such autonomy was an essential precondition for the lab to achieve its mandated objectives However, the army never imagined that Khan would abuse the trust and confidence reposed in him by the state. Furthermore, Khan gradually capitalized on his successes and the states mythologizing of his contributions to elevate himself to the status of a national hero. Hence, the organizational demands for success during the development phase of the nuclear weapons program, as well as Khans nearly unassailable position within domestic Pakistani politics, made it difficult for successive army chiefs to confront him for his transgressions.

Third, Musharraf maintains that the United States did not share intelligence on Khans proliferation network with the Pakistani government until very recently. In the absence of such damning evidence, it was difficult for the Pakistani government to proceed against Khan and his associates. And finally, Musharraf insists that the bulk of the proliferation from Pakistan occurred in the form of intellectual property transfers; the implication of his suggestion being that it is easier for governments to safeguard industrial hardware and nuclear material than the transmission of software.

The Counter Narrative

Musharrafs defense provides some useful information on the historical evolution of Pakistans nuclear command authority, the relationship between the military and the nuclear entities and scientists, and damning disclosures about Khans personal corruption, but it does not offer credible explanations as to how or why successive Pakistani governments remained ignorant of Khans activities for such a long period of time; or why they should not be held to account. On balance, the historical evidence points in the direction of a more complex and murkier reality that casts aspersions on Musharrafs motivations.

Admittedly, it is easier for governments to safeguard industrial hardware and equipment in comparison to software which resides in the neural networks of human beings, floppy disks, CDs, and computers. Humans can carry software on their person, unbeknownst to oversight authorities; and transmit it either verbally or electronically. However, evidence has surfaced that Khan and his associates proliferated both hardware and software. Pakistans Attorney General Makhdoom Ali Khan recently told the Rawalpindi bench of the Lahore High Court that the scientists transferred secret codes, nuclear materials, substances, machinery, equipment components, information, documents, sketches, plans, models, articles and notes entrusted them [scientists] in their official capacity. Given the logistics of moving machinery and materials, it is extraordinarily difficult to believe that the Pakistani military and its intelligence agencies had no inkling of the nuclear trade.

Musharraf has offered a novel explanation as to why the army did not know of the intimate happenings at KRL. According to him, the military commanders tasked with KRLs security detail were under the labs autonomous control; the military officers were answerable to Khan and not the army high command. However, most independent observers who are familiar with the Pakistani Armys professional ethics, training procedures, and command protocols are skeptical that this would indeed be the case. Others more familiar with KRLs security detail are equally dismissive of Musharrafs explanations.

Pakistani government sources have also suggested that KRLs security detail was designed to prevent penetration and sabotage of the nuclear weapons program from the outside. But it was not particularly well-designed to prevent the egress of men, material, and equipment in the reverse direction. The obvious flaw of designing a one-dimensional security model apart, the nature of nuclear cooperation with Iran and North Korea suggests that sensitive nuclear facilities in Pakistan were penetrated from the outside; and the osmosis of technical exchange between the scientists and entities was facilitated by formal nuclear cooperation agreements between the Pakistani and Iranian and later

North Korean governments.

Iranian nuclear scientists reportedly traveled to the port city of Karachi in Pakistan for technical briefings during the early 1990s.The ease with which foreign scientists and technicians gained access to Pakistani scientists and sensitive facilities stands in sharp contrast to the difficulty former Prime Minister Benazir Bhutto encountered while trying to gain similar access. For example, the army denied Bhutto security clearances to visit KRL during her first tenure as prime minister (1988-1990). General (retd.) Mirza Aslam Beg allegedly withheld details about the nuclear weapons program from the prime minister on the rationale that briefings at Kahuta were on a need-to-know basis. In another episode in 1979, the French ambassador to Pakistan was physically manhandled by Pakistani security forces when he made the mistake of venturing close to KRL. Thus, some of the anecdotal evidence from the late 1970s and early 1990s undercuts the armys recent assertions about lapses in KRLs security network.

Two former cabinet ministers in the first Nawaz Sharif government (1990-1993), Senator Ishaq Dar and Chaudhry Nisar Ali Khan have stated for the record that in 1991 former Chief of Army Staff General (retd.) Mirza Aslam Beg lobbied Sharif for the transfer of nuclear technology to a friendly state, for the sum of $12 billion. The proposed figure was apparently supposed to underwrite Pakistans defense budget for the decade.According to Dar, a representative of that friendly state accompanied Beg when he made the offer. However, Sharif, rejected Begs proposal.

Similarly, Nisar Ali Khan maintains that in the aftermath of the 1991 Gulf War, Beg proposed that Pakistan should sell its nuclear technology to Iran as part of a grand alliance. The generals reasoning: that after the United States succeeded in defeating Iraq, it might be the turn of Iran and Pakistan next. Sharif, according to Nisar, rejected Begs proposal. But this does not rule out the possibility that Khan and Beg might have acted independently of the prime minister, who never had control over the nuclear weapons program in any case.

Musharrafs protestation to the contrary, Pakistani governments have had some knowledge about Khans activities and about equipment and technology transfers from KRL to Iran and North Korea. There is evidence to suggest that every army chief from the late 1980s has known of Tehrans interest in acquiring enrichment technologies from Pakistan for a weapons program. Apparently, Pakistani investigators have also found evidence that Khan informed Beg of equipment transfers to Iran. However, Beg claims that he received assurances from Khan that the equipment being sold to the Iranians was outmoded and disused and would not enable them to enrich uranium in the short term.

Washington has also raised proliferation concerns with Islamabad repeatedly since the early 1990s. Former US Ambassador to Pakistan Robert B. Oakley (1988-1991) recalls Beg telling him in 1991 that he had reached an understanding with the head of Irans Revolutionary Guards to help Tehran with its nuclear program in return for an oil facility and conventional weapons. An alarmed Oakley broached the subject with Prime Minister Nawaz Sharif. Subsequently, according to Oakley, Sharif and Pakistani President Ghulam Ishaq Khan informed the Iranian government that Pakistan would not carry such an agreement through.

In the mid-1990s, when UNSCOM inspectors in Iraq uncovered documentary proof that Khan had approached Saddam Husseins regime with offers of assistance in the area of centrifuge-based uranium enrichment, the Pakistani government declared that it had conducted an internal investigation and found the allegations to be fraudulent.

Similarly, Washington began querying Islamabad about possible nuclear transfers to North Korea as early as 1998. Musharraf also recently confirmed that the ISI raided an aircraft bound for North Korea in 2000 after it was tipped off that KRL was transferring sensitive equipment to Pyongyang; but that raid drew a blank. More recently, US State Department spokesperson Richard Boucher took issue with Musharrafs charge that Washington did not provide the Pakistani government with timely intelligence against Khan; Boucher insisted that the United States had discussed nonproliferation issues with Pakistan repeatedly, over a long period of time, and its been an issue of concern to us and President Musharraf...so its not a single moment of information.

Besides the intelligence inputs that Islamabad received from Washington, whistle blowers within the Pakistani nuclear establishment began warning the Pakistani military and its intelligence agencies about Khans corruption as early as the late 1980s. Musharraf recently admitted that he suspected Khan of clandestine proliferation activities as early as 1998; and that it was a critical factor behind his removal from KRL in March 2001.Yet, despite Khans removal, US intelligence tracked strategic trade between Pakistan and North Korea until fall 2002. More alarmingly, Khan and his network coordinated nuclear trade with Libya until October 2003; and Khan, despite being moved out of KRL, was able to transfer a nuclear weapons design to Libya in late 2001 or early 2002.

But oddly enough, despite mounting evidence that Khan might have profited illegally by selling the Pakistani states most sensitive secrets, the Pakistani military did not consider it fit to investigate him or his top associates until

October 2003. Despite repeated foreign government entreaties, published documentary evidence, foreign intelligence leaks, and news reports alleging nuclear proliferation to Iran and North Korea over a period of 14 years, the proverbial Pakistani military watchdog did not bark. Furthermore, even after the Pakistani government launched an internal probe after receiving incriminating intelligence from the United States and the IAEA in fall 2003, Pakistani investigators visited Iran, Libya, Dubai, and Malaysia, but excluded North Korea from their itinerary.

The Pakistani militarys lack of institutional curiosity in investigating the internal affairs of its nuclear scientists and labs, physical transfers of machinery, nuclear materials, and components from Pakistan over land routes and on board chartered and air force transports, travel of Pakistani scientists to Iran, and training/briefing sessions for Iranian and North Korean scientists in Pakistan, suggests that the Musharraf regime is being frugal with the truth. In fact, Musharraf alluded to the latter reality in an address to Pakistani journalists when he said that even if for the sake of argument it were accepted that the Pakistani military and governments were involved in nuclear proliferation, the Pakistani press should avoid debating the issue out of deference to the countrys national interests.

Washingtons Muted Response

Washingtons public reaction to what is perhaps the greatest proliferation scandal in history has been relatively muted. Although US officials have privately expressed disbelief that such massive diversions from KRL could have occurred for nearly two decades without the knowledge and consent of the Pakistani military, the Bush administration has publicly accepted Musharrafs fiction that Khans was a rogue operation; and that the Pakistani military and other state functionaries were probably unaware of some of Khans operations. Senior administration officials have also publicly lauded President Musharraf for investigating Khan and his associates and strengthening internal controls over KRL.

However, Washington has privately warned Musharraf that Pakistan risks jeopardizing the $3 billion proposed economic aid package and its relations with the United States. During a visit to Islamabad in October 2003, US Deputy Secretary of State Richard Armitage personally presented evidence against Khan to Musharraf and threatened that Pakistan could be reported to the United Nations Security Council and suffer sanctions if it failed to put an end to Khans nuclear entrepreneurship permanently. The implicit bargain between Washington and Islamabad: the United States will avoid publicly hectoring and embarrassing Musharraf in return for a Pakistani undertaking to tear up Khans clandestine nuclear trading network from its roots; intelligence inputs that would help US intelligence agencies fill critical gaps in their knowledge about the scale, depth, and *modus operandi* of the clandestine global trade in nuclear technologies; and details on North Korea and possibly Irans uranium enrichment programs.

Washingtons public nonchalance has also been determined by the necessity of avoiding actions that might rebound on Musharraf domestically. The Bush administration regards Musharraf and the Pakistani Army as critical allies in the global war on terror against al-Qaeda and the Taliban. Since the launch of the Afghan war in fall 2001, Pakistan has rendered critical intelligence, logistical, and military support for US military operations. Pakistans cooperation has also been critical in apprehending al-Qaeda operatives taking shelter in Pakistan and along the Pakistan-Afghan border. Because Osama Bin Laden and his key lieutenants remain at large, and because the United States needs Pakistans political support to pacify the resurgent Taliban threat in Afghanistan, the Bush administration has resorted to quiet diplomacy to force changes in Islamabads proliferation policies.

In this regard, re-imposition of US economic sanctions would only compound the problem. On the one hand, because the drivers that led to Pakistani proliferation in the past would remain in place, economic privation would only create further incentives for the Pakistani military to feed its corporate appetite through weapons of mass destruction-related technology sales abroad. On the other hand, the consequences of military action against Pakistan would be infinitely worse. If the United States ever made the mistake of degrading or destroying the Pakistani militarys coercive capacity, Pakistan might become a failed state, and the problem of securing its nuclear facilities, fissile materials, scientific personnel, and actual weapons and delivery systems would become a security nightmare.

Because it is likely that some of past clandestine nuclear trade had the tacit if not formal support of the Pakistani military, the United States is also perhaps trying to avoid actions that would place Musharraf, who is also the head of the army, in an institutional quandary. Perhaps the quiet calculation in Washington is that a policy of selective intelligence leaks, private and multilateral diplomacy, and a combination of carrots and sticks would constitute more robust means to persuade Islamabad to mend its ways. More enticing is the possibility, howsoever remote, of recruiting the Pakistani militarys intelligence agencies and nuclear labs to help roll up the global black market in nuclear technologies they helped create in the first place.

Finally, the US reticence in publicly rebuking Islamabad for its proliferation transgressions is an acknowledgement of the sensitive regard with which nuclear issues are treated in domestic Pakistani politics. Nuclear weapons are closely tied to the Pakistani nations sense of self-worth and national identity. Pakistanis count their nuclear capability as one of the few areas of national achievement. Nuclear scientists are treated as cult figures; and until recently, the Pakistani state lionized Khan as a national hero. Khan and the nuclear establishment also enjoy the support of the Islamist parties in Pakistan. Hence, Washington has been keen to avoid giving the impression that it is intruding into the holy sanctum of Pakistans nuclear politics; or doing anything that would compromise Pakistans nuclear weapons program. But, behind the façade of public calm, US policy makers have launched a quiet program of cooperation to help Pakistan institute more reliable personnel reliability protocols, and enhance the safety and security of its nuclear warheads, fissile materials, and sensitive nuclear facilities.

Preliminary Conclusions

Without a doubt, the new revelations show that Pakistan remains the most problematic nuclear state in the international system and perhaps the state of greatest proliferation concern. KRLs diversion of centrifuge blueprints, designs, models, complete assemblies, components, enriched uranium, and the actual design of a warhead itself without a nary afterthought of the likely political consequences of such actions, is unparalleled in the history of nuclear proliferation.

In the mid-1970s and 1980s, Pakistans nuclear weapons program presented a new model of proliferation. In the past, state-to-state cooperation had been the main conduit for the passage of nuclear weapons-related technologies. However, Pakistani entrepreneurs such as A.Q. Khan demonstrated how loose export control regulations, dual-use technologies, market ethics, and a fragmented manufacturing base spread across different countries could be exploited by a determined proliferators to build an integrated fissile material production complex. The Pakistanis perfected a system of clandestine trade through middlemen and shell companies; through clandestine procurement techniques, false end-user certificates, and diversion of industrial goods and technologies placed on the export control lists of advanced industrial nations using circuitous routes. But that effort took about a decade to accomplish.

In comparison, new proliferators such as North Korea and Libya have been able to reduce substantially the lead time for setting up similar facilities. Libya, for example, was able to set up a pilot uranium enrichment plant within five years; and could have conceivably extracted enough enriched uranium for a single nuclear weapon on a crash basis. The critical difference between the Pakistani and North Korean and Libyan cases is that the latter tapped into the services of nuclear entrepreneurs such as Khan who provided a one-stop shop for uranium enrichment programs: integrated shopping solutions for complete centrifuge assemblies; component parts and manufacturing services; enriched uranium; engineering consultancies and trouble shooting services; and finally the blueprint of an actual fission weapon itself. Thus the same fragmented network that fed the Pakistani nuclear weapons effort morphed into what IAEA Director General Mohamed ElBaradei described as an underground international WalMart for nuclear weapons technologies.

Any analysis of the proliferators motivations will have to wait until we have a more definitive idea of whether Khans activities were entirely a rogue operation or conducted at the behest of the Pakistani military. Revelations of Khans disproportionate wealth and the *modus operandi* of his associates clearly suggest that money was a primary motivation. But Khan has also justified his actions as means to help other Muslim nations and divert Western attention and pressure from the Pakistani nuclear weapons program. However his sales to secular regimes in North Korea and Libya, and offers to other secular regimes in Syria and Iraq suggest that although ideology and antipathy to the West might have played some role, it was in part a cover to mask his greed and megalomania.

Although the Pakistani government has distanced itself from Khans activities, it is difficult to believe that a diversion of such massive scale and scope over a period of nearly two decades could have occurred without the knowledge of oversight authorities within the Pakistani government. Evidently, Khan made nuclear transfers to Iran under the rubric of a secret peaceful nuclear cooperation agreement that the two countries signed in the mid-1980s. The historical record shows that former Pakistani president, the late General Zia-ul-Haq, was aware of Irans interest in purchasing Pakistani enrichment technology that would enable it to enrich uranium to weapons grade. The historical record is equally clear that General (retd.) Beg, who immediately succeeded Zia, toyed with the idea of nuclear technology sales to finance

Pakistans defense budget. Khan also informed Beg of the equipment sales to Iran. However, Beg insists that Khan had assured him that the equipment being sold was outmoded, old, and disused, and would not enable Tehran to enrich uranium in the near term. Similarly, the Musharraf regime has never admitted to Nodong imports from North Korea or explained how it cobbled together the resources to pay for them.

But there is also the possibility that the Pakistani military approved transfers of a limited scope and nature to Iran and North Korea; but that Khan and his associates abused the authority granted them to make unauthorized sales of goods and services and reap huge personal financial rewards in the process. However, the Musharraf regimes attempt to absolve the Pakistani state of all blame in the current controversy by suggesting that Pakistani scientists acted out of pecuniary and career goals borders on the preposterous. If the above argument were accepted in principal, no future government in Islamabad could be held accountable for transfers or theft of fissile material, warheads, or other weapons-related technologies and know how from Pakistan. By Musharrafs logic, Khan and his associates could have also diverted weapons-grade uranium or an actual nuclear weapon itself to foreign clients and the Pakistani military would claim innocence. Even if the nuclear entities and scientists were acting independently, the Pakistani state is ultimately responsible for the guardianship of all nuclear assets, technologies, and personnel on its territory.

Although Islamabads proliferation record raises serious concerns, the current Pakistani governments assertion that its scientists and entities might have acted at cross purposes and in a manner unbeknownst to state authorities, is infinitely worse. For the record would then suggest that not only did civilian governments in Islamabad lack effective control over the nuclear weapons program during its developmental phase, but that the military too, which analysts believe effectively monitors the nuclear weapons effort, exercised only perfunctory control. The implications of such abdication of internal sovereignty by the state are staggering. It suggests that behind the façade of centralized control, Pakistans strategic military-industrial complex is dangerously fragmented, compartmentalized, and autonomous; that government agencies lack effective oversight; and individuals act as authorities unto themselves. In light of their alleged past behavior, the possibility that such individuals might share secrets concerning the dark nuclear arts with other countries and terror groups for ideological and financial motivations is not as remote as it had once seemed.

Irans and Libyas revelations about their Pakistani connection are also likely to have a sobering effect on other proliferators in the international system. Proliferator states, rogue entities, scientists, engineers, manufacturers and suppliers can no longer feel assured that their identities will be protected by client states. Tripoli and Tehrans acts have also undermined the Pakistani Islamists a historic notions of an imagined pan-Islamic community of Muslim nations. During a press conference, Musharraf raged that Pakistan had been ousted by its Muslim brothers with whom it had shared its most sensitive defense technologies; and such treachery is the reason why Pakistanis should abandon chimeras of an Islamic bomb.

Equally significant, the disclosure that Khan and his associates sold the blueprint of a nuclear weapon design, which the Chinese had shared with Pakistan, to Libya and possibly Iran and North Korea, is likely to embarrass China. It confirms what was known for a long time; that

China helped Pakistan with the design for nuclear weapons. But despite the obvious strain on Sino-Pakistani relations, it remains unclear whether the new disclosures will lead Beijing to reappraise its decision to continue help for Pakistans solid-fuel ballistic missile and possibly nuclear programs.

Finally, although Pakistan can be expected to provide some intelligence inputs to help root out the clandestine international network in nuclear trade, the extent of its cooperation is likely to be limited. For Islamabads own nuclear weapons and ballistic missile programs have profited from such trade; and remain dependent on it. Recently, a South African businessman was discovered trying to illegally export triggered spark gaps that can be used in nuclear weapons to Pakistan through false end-user certification. This episode is a small indicator of just how far Pakistan is from achieving self-sufficiency.

Worse, most of the drivers that led Pakistani entities such as KRL to proliferate nuclear technologies in the past remain. Khans greed was only one variable in the proliferation equation. Other drivers such as the Pakistani militarys corporate appetite for a nuclear deterrent and maintaining proportional parity with their larger and more powerful neighbor India, are constants in the Pakistani political spectrum. Domestically as well, Pakistans institutions remain relatively undeveloped. Individuals dominate institutional processes; there is little respect for the rule of law or constitution; and critical sectors such as the nuclear weapons and ballistic missile programs remain beyond the pale of civilian oversight. It was this combination of factors - the militarys corporate desperation for nuclear and missile deliverables, undeveloped institutions, personalization of power, fragmented and compartmentalized authority structures, and the absence of civilian oversight - that provided opportunities for Khan and his associates to peddle their dangerous wares in the international market. Although the Pakistani Army appears to be making efforts to tighten its grip on the nuclear and missile military-industrial complex, the larger structural problems in the Pakistani polity remain. And it is this combination of factors that might pave the way for a similar recurrence in the future. It is also why Pakistan will require careful monitoring and reform and remain one of the most significant foreign policy challenges for the United States in the near and medium term.

An Example of How Libya Acquired Gas Centrifuges from the A.Q. Khan Nuclear Black Market

1. A representative of a third-world country with nuclear aspirations, like Libya, makes contact with another regional power with similar religious fundamentalist elements and goals. (Between 1997 and 2002, representatives from Libya met with Pakistans chief nuclear scientist, A.Q. Khan, several times in Dubai, Istanbul, and Casablanca to discuss how Khan could assist with Libyas nuclear ambitions.)

2. Once contact is established with the black market network, the network then contacts the necessary middlemen. (The Khan nuclear network relied heavily on a Sri Lankan middleman, Buhary Syed Abu Tahir, based out of Malaysia, to keep the network organized and operational.)

3.   Operating through legitimate front companies, the network uses one front company to place an order for the necessary equipment needed to manufacture the components for the centrifuges. (Peter Griffin, a British national, places an order for his company, Gulf Technical Industries (GTI), part of parent company Scomi Group, on behalf of the Khan smuggling network.)

4.   The legitimate front company places an order with another legitimate front company in the network for several consignments of dual-use machinery. (Scomi Precision Engineering [SCOPE], a division of the Scomi Group, creates the Malaysian division of Scomi Engineering in 2001 expressly to machine the necessary components. Scomi is principally owned by Kaspadu Investment Holding Company, a company whose director is none other than Buhary Syed Tahir, the primary middleman in the Khan nuclear network.)

5.   Basing itself in a country with lax export regulations and practices, the production company creates the components and ships them to the ordering company. (SCOPE ships four consignments of centrifuge components from Kuala Lumpur to GTI in Dubai.)

6.   After being received by the ordering company, the components are then relabeled as less conspicuous items and shipped via transportation that does not have a port of call from the country of either the production company or the ordering company. (The

consignments shipped from SCOPE/Malaysia to GTI/Dubai were disguised and relabeled to avoid detection; at the 2003 Suez Canal interdiction of components to Libya, the shipping manifest listed the 40-foot long containers as used machine parts.)

7.   Upon receipt of the components, the client gains the necessary expertise from the network to first machine the non-importable parts in the client country and then assemble and operate the uranium enrichment centrifuges. (Plans were made to create a workshop in Libya to construct the centrifuge components that could not be obtained outside of the country.)

Timeline of Events in A.Q. Khans Nuclear Network and the Democratic Peoples Republic of Korea (DPRKs) Nuclear Program

- **1970s:** A.Q. Khan worked at Urenco, a British-Dutch nuclear consortium, in Holland. During this time, Khan smuggled plans for a gas centrifuge enrichment process to Pakistan.
- **1976:** Khan founds the Engineering Research Laboratory (ERL).
- **1981:** The ERL is renamed the Khan Research Laboratory (KRL).
- **1990s:** During the decade of the 1990s, A.Q. Khan visits the DPRK 13 times under the auspices of the Pakistani government.
- **1990:** A.Q. Khan receives Pakistans Man of the Nation award.

- **1992:** Khan initiates talks with North Korea to obtain intermediate-range ballistic missiles in return for gas centrifuge designs and other technical assistance.

- **1993:** Reportedly at the insistence of Khan, Pakistani Prime Minister Benazir Bhutto travels to North Korea to retrieve electronic files of missile designs.

- **1998:** Pakistan test-fires a 937-mile-range Ghauri missile, this missile, designed by A.Q. Khan, is based on the North Korean No-Dong, a version of the Scud missile.

- **1999:** During a visit, Khan claims to have seen three plutonium nuclear devices at an undisclosed North Korean location, approximately one hour north of Pyongyang.

- **2000:** At Pakistans first international arms exhibition in November, Khan Research Laboratory was present, openly offering brochures that advertised the availability of enrichment components as well as complete gas centrifuges.

- **2003:** In April, a cargo ship bound for North Korea was interdicted in the Suez Canal; it contained aluminum tubing that matched the specification for the centrifuge designs provided by Khan.

- **2004:** Khan, on Pakistani national television, admits heading a clandestine global network that trafficked illicit nuclear materials and know-how. Khan signs an affidavit stating that his network supplied the DPRK with drawings, sketches, technical data, and depleted uranium hexaflouride gas.

1987 Meeting Between Iran and AQ Khan Network

IAEA Deputy Director General Pierre Goldschmidts Statement to the Board of Governors confirms an account, which first appeared in *The Washington Post*, that the A.Q. Khan network offered Iran assistance with its centrifuge program in 1987.

Goldschmidt told the Board of Governors:

During a meeting on 12 January 2005 in Tehran, Iran showed the Agency a handwritten one-page document reflecting an offer said to have been made to Iran in 1987 by a foreign intermediary. While it is not entirely clear from the document precisely what the offer entailed, Iran has stated that it related to centrifuge technology acquisition. This document suggests that the offer included the delivery of: a disassembled sample machine (including drawings, descriptions, and specifications for production); drawings, specifications and calculations for a complete plant; and materials for 2000 centrifuge machines. The document also reflects an offer to provide auxiliary vacuum and electric drive equipment and uranium re-conversion and casting capabilities.

According to *The Washington Post*, the 1987 meeting took place in Dubai between three Iranian officials, a Sri Lankan businessman named Mohamed Farouq and a German named Heinz Mebus.

Iran claims enrichment has entered the industrial phase

During a ceremony on April 9 marking National Nuclear Day, Iran announced that its uranium enrichment work had entered the industrial phase. As Irans commercial-scale enrichment plant at Natanz is far from complete, the announcement appears to have been made more for political impact than to mark a true technical milestone in Irans quest to produce large quantities of enriched uranium. Most Iranian officials have not said explicitly that enrichment at the underground plant has begun—though the step is clearly not far off. By the end of March, Iran had reportedly installed six cascades of 164 centrifuges each, and was allegedly testing four of these cascades under vacuum. Iran had also moved 8.7 tons of uranium gas feedstock to the plant by the end of February.

Irans determined pursuit of uranium enrichment led the U.N. Security Council to ratchet up sanctions on March 24, with the unanimous adoption of Resolution 1747. This resolution builds on a previous Security Council resolution, passed last December, by expanding the list of Iranian entities subject to an asset freeze because of their involvement in Irans nuclear and missile work. To the nearly two dozen entities already named, 28 entities were added, including seven officials in the Revolutionary Guard Corps, several scientists at the Ministry of Defense, and subsidiary entities of the Atomic Energy Organization, the Aerospace Industries Organization and the Defense Industries Organization. Also included in the list—at the insistence of the United States—is Bank Sepah, one of Irans oldest and largest state-owned banks, which is accused of supporting Irans missile effort.

The only new mandatory penalty in this resolution bars Iran from exporting conventional arms and related materials. For the sake of maintaining Security Council unanimity, several key penalties were sacrificed: countries are only asked to exercise vigilance and restraint in transferring arms to Iran, and are called upon, but not required, to cut off grants, financial assistance, and concessional loans to the Iranian government. In addition, countries must report whether a person sanctioned by the Council has entered into or transited through their territory, but these persons are not subject to a travel ban.

Resolution 1747 and its predecessor, Resolution 1737, approved unanimously by the Security Council on December 23, call on Iran to suspend all enrichment, reprocessing and heavy water-related activities, to ratify the IAEAs Additional Protocol, and to implement transparency measures so that IAEA inspectors may resolve questions about Irans past nuclear work. Both resolutions were written under Article 41, Chapter VII of the U.N. Charter, which makes compliance mandatory and allows the United Nations to use economic and diplomatic measures—but not military force—to compel compliance.

Until it complies with U.N. demands, Iran is barred from importing or exporting most items related to uranium enrichment, reprocessing, heavy water activities and nuclear weapon delivery systems, and states are barred from providing Iran with financial or technical assistance aimed at acquiring these items. States must also to exercise vigilance in providing Iranian nationals with specialized nuclear and missile-related training.

In order to oversee implementation, the Security Council created a Committee composed of Council members, responsible for investigating alleged violations of the resolutions, for expanding the asset freeze and travel surveillance to additional entities, and for considering exemption requests.

IRANS SUSPECT ENTITIES

This page provides a database of Iranian entities - persons, companies, institutes, government agencies - that are thought to be contributing to Irans nuclear, chemical, or biological weapon capabilities or to its missiles or advanced conventional weapon programs. Every effort has been made to update the database regularly.

The information presented here has been collected from sources the Wisconsin Project believes to be reliable; however, the Wisconsin Project does not guarantee full accuracy or completeness.

IRANS SUPPLIERS

This page provides a database of entities - persons, companies, governments - that are thought to have supplied technology, equipment, material or expertise to Iran that would enhance Irans ability to construct nuclear, chemical, biological or advanced conventional weapons or long-range missiles.

The information presented here has been collected from sources the Wisconsin Project believes to be reliable; however, the Wisconsin Project does not guarantee full accuracy or completeness.

Abdul Qadeer Khan

Air Rig Inc. Aizaz Jaffery ANA Training Ltd. Andrew A. Adams, Equipment and Supply International Atomenergoproekt State Planning and Design, Research and Survey Institute Atomstroyexport

(ASE) Avtomatika Zavod (CKBA) Baltic State Technical University Beijing Institute of Aerodynamics (BIA) Beijing Institute of Geology Airborne Measurement and Remote Sensing Research Center Beijing Institute of Opto-Electronic Technology (BIOET) Beijing Research Institute of Uranium Geology (BRIUG) Belvneshpromservice Bharat Electronics Ltd. (BEL) Blagoja Samakoski Central Aerohydrodynamic Institute (TsAGI) Changgwang Sinyong Corporation Chen Qingchang (Chinese citizen) Cheong Yee Limited Chernyshev Moscow Machine Building Enterprise China Aerospace Science and Technology Corporation (CASC) China Great Wall Industry Corporation (CGWIC) China Machinery and Electric Equipment Import-Export Corporation China Machinery and Equipment Import-Export Corporation China National Aero-Technology Import-Export Corporation (CATIC) China National Electronics Import-Export Corporation (CEIEC) China National Machinery and Electric Equipment Import-Export Company China National Machinery and Equipment Import-Export Corporation China National Non-metallic Minerals Industrial Import and Export Corporation (CNMIEC) China National Non-metallic Minerals Industry Corporation (Group) (CNMC) China North Chemical Industries Corporation (NOCINCO) China North Industries Corporation (NORINCO) China Nuclear Energy Industry Corporation (CNEIC) China Precision Engineering Institute for Aircraft Industry (CPEI) China Precision Machinery Import-Export Corporation (CPMIEC) China Shipbuilding Trading Company (CSTC) Chinese Academy of Sciences (CAS) CMEC Machinery and Electric Equipment Import-Export Corporation (CMECMEE) CMEC Machinery and Electrical Import-Export Corporation Computer &

*Communicatii SRL Cuanta SA D. I. Mendeleyev
University of Chemical Technology (MUCT) D. V.
Efremov Scientific Research Institute of Electrophysical
Apparatus David Chu Dr. C. Surendar Dr. Y. S. R.
Prasad Eddie Johansson Elektrosila Elmstone Service
and Trading FZE (LLC) En-Wei Eric Chang Europalace
2000 Eva-Marie Hack Experimental Design Bureau
Hydropress GBC Scientific Equipment Pty Ltd.
Glavkosmos Goodly Industrial Company Ltd. Gotthard
Lerch Harold Hemming Heli-World Aviation, Ltd.
Industrial Scientific Corporation (ISC) Inor Institute of
Industrial Control Systems (IICS) Institute of Reactor
Materials (IRM) Izhora Plant Joint-Stock Company Jabal
Damavand General Trading Company Jami S.
Choudhury Jetpower Industrial, Ltd. Jiangsu Yongli
Chemical Engineering and Technology Import-Export
Corporation Joint Stock Company Atommash Joint Stock
Company Leningradsky Metallichesky Zavod (LMZ)
Khazra Trading Liao Minglong (Chinese citizen) LIMMT
Economic and Trade Company, Ltd. Liyang Chemical
Equipment Company Lizen Open Joint Stock Company
Mercator, Inc. Mikrosam Moscow Aviation Institute
(MAI) Moscow Bauman State University of Technology
Moso Moso (now defunct) N.A. Dollezhal Research and
Development Institute of Power Engineering (NIKIET)
Nanjing Chemical Industries Group (NCI) NEC
Engineers Nuclear Power Corporation of India Ltd.
(NPCIL) Omsk Baranov Motor-Building Production
Association Oriental Scientific Instruments Import and
Export Corporation (OSIC) Otto Heilingbrunner
Pakistan Aeronautical Complex (PAC) Pan Yongming
(Chinese citizen) Pars Company Inc. Polyus Scientific
Production Association Projects and Development India,
Ltd. (PDIL) Prometey Central Scientific Research*

Institute of Structural Materials Rallis India Refinery Industries Rex International Development Ricks Manufacturing Rosoboronexport Rotair Industries Incorporated Sargsian, Armen (Armenian citizen) Seishin Enterprise Co., Ltd. Selenergoproekt Joint Stock Company (AOOT ROSEP) Shao Xingsheng (Chinese citizen) State Research Institute of Graphite - Based Structural Materials (NIIGrafit) Sukhoi Design Bureau Aviation Scientific Industrial Complex Summit Marketing, Inc. Taian Foreign Trade General Corporation (TFT) Techsnabexport Foreign Economic Joint Stock Company Telstar Tian Yi (Chinese citizen) Transpek Industry Limited Trud State Scientific Production Association Ulan-Ude Aircraft Aviation Plant Joint Stock Company Vadim Vorobey Vladov, Mikhail Pavlovich (Moldovan citizen) Wha Cheong Tai Company William W. Manning, Camnetics Manufacturing Corp. Zaporizhzhya Regional Foreign Economic Association Zibo Chemical Equipment Plant (ZCEP)

United States and Operation Merlin

Under Executive Order 13292 signed March 25th 2003 US classifies secret under Confidential, Secret, Top Secret, Beyond Top Secret. A special Access Program Operation Merlin was so sensitive that clearance for this type of covert operation must come from very highest level of government. Both President Clinton and George W. Bush approved it. In 2000 the CIA US intelligence agencies were beginning to zero in on A.Q. Khans network and its sale of Nuclear Secrets to Iran, CIA was able to penetrate this network and learn that there really was a lot going on. The CIA came up with an plan to derail Irans Nuclear Weapons

Research Operation Merlin was one to the most secretive operation during that time, the plan according to highly placed intelligence sources was to pass flawed Nuclear designs to Iran, and if they tried to build a nuclear weapon it would be a dud. Setting them back in their Nuclear program several years. To carry out the operation the CIA hand picked a former Soviet scientist who had worked at Arzumas 16 the Soviet Los Alamos before defecting to the United States. This scientist had been working for the CIA as an asset but he had never done anything like this before. He was reluctant at first and felt this was more than he ever bargained for. They met with him in in a hotel in San Francisco, where they briefed him and handed over the designs, the designs were actual blue prints for a firing set a critical component of a Nuclear Weapon. They also had brought in Nuclear experts from one of the national laboratories to embed the flaws into the design where no one was able to tell. The Russian scientist immediately spotted the flaws and voiced his opinion that the Iranian would do the same. The senior officials at CIA did not care that he saw the flaws and decided to ignore it, this in my opinion was as serious problem in this operation. His assignment was to go to Vienna find the Iranian attending a meeting with the IAEA and hand deliver these blue prints posing as an unemployed Nuclear scientist from Russia who had stolen these blue prints. He walked around aimlessly in Vienna for two days possibly because he was nervous and unsure if he wanted to go through with the assignment. Finally he saw a mail carrier delivering mail and figured this was the best way, but in carrying out the mission the Russian scientist double crossed the CIA fearing the Iranian will come after him for passing bad information, he enclosed a letter indicating that there were problems with the blue prints.

According to the intelligence sources this is what he actually wrote *If you try to create a similar device you will need to ask some practical questions.*

There is some US intelligence that the Iranians went back to Tehran with the blue prints but there is no evidence what happen after that. It is quite possible it in fact aided the Iranian because there was so much information in there that was valid as oppose to flawed. No one knows the Russian scientist fate.

Mossad and MEK[Mujahedin-e-Khalq Organization]

CIA wasnt the only intelligence agency infiltrating Iran, the Israels secret intelligence the Mossad desperately needed to know how close Iran was to building a Nuclear weapon, Mossad has a number of operations which one of them was called Operation Soft-Shoe where the Mossad agents had to collect soil samples, some sources say this is how the Natanz Nuclear Power Plant was exposed, though the Mossad decided they didnt want to be known for having this information so they passed it on the Iranian resistance group MEK this is Irans main opposition network who have their members uniquely placed in key positions in the Iranian regime. MEK pumped its contacts in construction industry in Iran and came up with revealing evidence. It was known that there was a shortage of concrete because so much of it was being absorbed by Natanz.

With its top secret information MEK helped Alireza Jafarzadeh and Iranian defector and a US MEK spokesman to blow the lid off of Iranian Nuclear ambitions. In august of 2002 Alireza made a stunning announcement which revealed exact location of Nuclear Site, and individuals involved in it. **Message delivered in Spring of 2007**

In the spring of 2007 the US sent Iran a warning of what could happen if it continued its Nuclear Weapons Program. The US positioned two giants aircraft carriers and their strike group on station in the Persian Gulf in the waters off Iran. You have to imagine that they have received this message. Sources say along with this United States have been waging war on another front a clandestine war, deep inside Iran to destabilize the Mullahs regime and topple Ahmedinejad by special operations deploying them through Pakistan using the Baluchis and Kurds who have ties to the Kurds in Iraq.

Military Strike by Israel

The Israelis have been working on a military strike on Iran for a decade now, I believe they are fully capable of doing this alone. Back in the 90s they have been buying F-15I and recently F-16I these are long range aircrafts. This is very possible for Israel because it has done this in the past in 1981 when Israel targeted the Crown Jewel of Iraqs Nuclear Program the above ground Osarek Nuclear Reactor at Twetha. Israel had decent intelligence and knew when to strike, the idea was to strike before their program would go hot, they had redlined it to avoid a nuclear accident. The Osarek raid damaged the reactor to the point that it couldnt be repaired, it destroyed the Core and the Containment dome.

The Iranians have learned quite a bit from the Osarek raid, thats why they have multiple facilities spread out wide across their country. That is why their Centrifuge facility is underground. Some sources believe that if Israel were to strike it would be one of the three targets number one Natanz a Uranium Enrichment Facility a very hardened target, it is buried very deeply, reports are under 8 meters of concrete, it has thick walls, this was built with the idea that it would be attacked. Natanz has two primary sites a Pilot Fuel Enrichment Plant Which is above ground and an underground Hall that designed to house 50 thousand Uranium Enriching Centrifuges. September 2007 President Ahmedinejad boasted he had 3000 active Centrifuges, the number could be lower. Pakistan had a lower number of Centrifuges when they build their first bomb. Arak the next target this site has reactor which could be advantageous in producing Plutonium, a Heavy Water Production facility. The third target Isfahan above ground Nuclear site main target there is a Uranium Conversion facility. This target is difficult because it is in the middle of other buildings, this will hurt both production routes Uranium and Plutonium.

If Iran gets bombed it would strike back both at Israel and United States, under those circumstances it makes sense to do the best job possible.

United States Military Strike

Usually when you have contingency plans you have multiple contingency plans, the danger in going to attack Iran light plan would be you have to assume they wont strike back, I think that would be a huge assumption. The most credible contingency plan is the more robust one, huge number of air and cruise missile strikes

Natanz by far is the most difficult to attack in terms of its size and the fact that it is buried under two feet of concrete in a bunker style complex, but it may not withstand the latest US weapon the largest bunker buster yet a thirty thousand pound monster called the Massive Ordnance Penetrator, carried by a Stealth bomber or a B-52 it has ten time the explosive power than its predecessors. First taking out their retaliatory capabilities, their sea skimming missiles, other anti-ship missiles all around the strait of Hermuz and the Island in the Persian Gulf, their scud capabilities, their speed boat fleet they trained to swarm around commercial and military shipping. If the attack is executed we could attack Iran from five different places, Air bases in Iraq , from the Gulf strike aircraft carriers, heavy bomber operating out of Diego Garcia and ballistic missiles from submarines in the Red sea and the Gulf area. It would take well over a thousand sorties and a very complex operation to say the least. Their center piece of air defense system are over thirty year old, we sold these to the Shah of Iran they are the improved Hawk surface to air missiles. What is of concern is the newer system SA-15 which the Russian recently sold to Iran. If the United States decides to attack the suspected sites of Iran the window of opportunity is small, because if Iran completes its Uranium Enrichment it could cause a disaster rather than avoiding one. An attack on Natanz when the Centrifuges are full of UF6 could potentially release tons of Uranium Hexafluoride in the atmosphere which is both toxic and radioactive. Not to do anything has its own set of problems and history would say it was George Bushs fault the Iranians went Atomic on his watch it was too late when the other President came in. In my opinion best time for military action is late fall and winter these are prime months because the nights are longer. As I mentioned before Mahmud Ahmedinejad who subscribes to a fundamentalist arm of the Shia sect that envisions the end of the World may see such an attack as inevitable.

Chapter **12**
Iranian retaliation scenarios

I ran is preparing for revenge, their military is basically playground level. The other scenarios are a cause for concern and should be taken seriously, Iran has a Secret Network of Spies all around the Middle East, basically sleeper cells who have been planted there for year now by Iran, these are individuals who were recruited and brought to Iran for training by the regime and sent back and are further waiting instruction or signal from their bosses in Iran. Remember these are all fundamentalist and will not hesitate in anyway, according to some Iranian defectors these individual are regular folks school teacher, doctors, and such. It is safe to assume their signal would be an attack on Iran. For this we would need cooperation from all the governments in and around the Middle East. Iran will use Hezbollah which has cells all over the world including the United States, you might remember in the recent past there were arrest made in Charlotte, North Carolina a man name Mohammed Hamud by the FBI who found out he had links to Hezbollah leader Hasan Nasrullah, the cell was caught smuggling cigarettes from North Carolina where the taxes are low and selling them in Detroit Michigan where there are higher taxes.

The profits were sent to Lebanon to their boss. Hezbollah will activate its cells to attack the Economic Infrastructure by targeting US businesses abroad , US diplomatic facilities, which could lead to chaos around the world. The border to Iraq is wide open, the Iranian will send thousands of Revolutionary Guards US forces directly and could close down the supply line that keep the US forces alive. As American forces were moving in to Bagdad back in 2003 the Revolutionary Guards were sending their soldiers in covertly right behind the American and British forces, so the have already positioned their soldiers in key areas assuming an attack by the United States. They have militia friendly to them who will try to interfere with oil shipping.

I am positive Ahmedinejad has already started to consult with a man name Imad Fayez Mugniyah some call him the Mozart of terrorism this man was involved in the kidnapping of American in Beirut and bombing of US embassy in 1983 and 1984 this terrorist has killed more Americans abroad than anyone I know and he still walks free.

Lending even a small amount of radioactive waste in the form of a dirty bomb to either of those groups, not to mention any other radical Islamic group the nation at least supports ideologically, would change the face of this conflict and should rightly be considered when discussing whether striking Irans nuclear facilities is in our best interests. This is not necessarily a debate of should we keep Iran from obtaining a bomb, the nation already has radioactive waste and with the announcement it will increase uranium enrichment more radioactive waste will be produced.

While a dirty bomb would create havoc wherever one is detonated, it is still a small type attack when compared to a suitcase nuke or a nuclear weapon. This is an important distinction to make because a dirty bomb would not do the damage to Israel that Iran seeks, and there is a religious belief it is the duty of the Islamic Republic of Iran to destroy Israel.

I believe Iran would have no hesitation sending a nuclear warhead into Tel Aviv because it is Iranian President Mahmoud Ahmadinejads firm belief he must wipe out Israel to pave the path for the return of the 12th Imam. It is his religious fanaticism that is alarming and needs to be considered while his nation continues their pursuit for nuclear weapons. Unfortunately many naysayers fail to even bring this up in discussion perhaps because we dont fully understand the role of the 12th Imam and Ahmadinejads own belief he is one of the chosen people to help the 12th Imam return, but we must begin to.

That said, there are many Islamic religious structures in Israel that certainly would at least be damaged in such an attack. Would the nation that wants to be the center of the Islamic world risk damaging where Mohammed ascended into Heaven to sit by Allah?

Contrary to what is constantly being reported, Ahmadinejads own statements confirm his quest to destroy Israel, but Israels destruction must come after the United States has been put to the side. At a conference in Tehran dubbed The World without Zionism, the imagery that was widely reported and republished included a globe bearing the markings of the Star of David, which is of course also the markings of the nation of Israel, falling from the rest of the world. Cropped from most pictures was that a globe bearing the American flag was already on the ground and broken as Israels globe was falling.

This symbolism of taking down Israel after the United States however isnt the only evidence Ahmadinejad seeks to destroy the United States first. Also at the same conference Ahmadinejad proclaimed to those who doubt, to those who ask is it possible, or those who do not believe, I say accomplishment of a world without America and Israel is both possible and feasible. It is this reasoning that I believe Iran wont immediately strike Israel but rather they would strike the United States if the nation acquires a nuclear weapon. Iran knows any attack on Israel would be met with swift retribution by the United States. It must therefore end the Americans from protecting the State of Israel before it can once and for all pave the way for the 12th Imam to return the to the world.

In the religious battle of good versus evil the imagery of Satan is strong, and so too in Shia Islam is the imagery of the 12th Imam returning to the Earth. To those unfamiliar with the concept of the 12th Imam, think any other religious end of days scenario that involved a prophet, the son of God or any other religious entity reappearing to punish those who do not believe and reward those who do.

To some of us, this type of scenario is nothing more than a story passed down through time and warped through the many translations and interpretations all religious texts have been through. To others, the religion we worship is right and the end of days scenario written in our religious texts is accurate.

But theres a huge difference with those that believe our end of days scenario is accurate and the end of days belief of Ahmadinejad. Most Christians who are proclaiming this is the end of life on Earth or that the end is near dont actually feel that it is their duty to accelerate the end of days. As many end of days sites as there are on the Internet, very few actually state they want the end to come now, but rather they are exposing what they believe are the signs towards that advancement.

On the other hand, Ahmadinejad is a student of a religious belief that God wants his followers to wage war for his own fancies and die in his name; it is that belief that treasures death more than life. When he is not dropping notes to the 12th Imam who has been hiding in a well near Qom, Iran for centuries, Ahmadinejad is shining in divine light at the United Nations. Not only does Ahmadinejad feel he is chosen to help the return of the 12th Imam, he feels it is his duty and these notes he tosses down the well indicate he is trying to help the 12th Imam return.

The government of Iran only knows religion and feels their own nations quests are predetermined in an effort do Allahs bidding on this Earth. So while we as a nation and as an international community have now seemingly resigned ourselves to the fact Iran is a nuclear nation and while at least some diplomats, journalists and so-called pundits are resigned to Iran acquiring nuclear weapons, we need to shift our discussion to whether Iran will use a nuclear weapon and if so, where would one be aimed.

I certainly believe Iran would use a nuclear weapon for the leaders of Iran, it is their religious duty to do so, and from the statements made by Ahmadinejad, I feel the United States will be the first hit in an effort to make the United States impotent in defending Irans short-term religious goal which is the destruction of Israel. While other nations including Saudi Arabia realize Irans nuclear weapons wont only be pointed towards Tel Aviv, the same quieted condemnation out of the Middle East of Ahmadinejads wipe Israel off the map statements at The World without Zionism conference will likely be heard, or not heard of course, if Iran were to strike Israel first. There is no better target for Iran to strike that would strike up the religious fanaticism the nation exudes than to strike Israel, but it must first eliminate the Americans from protecting the state of Israel.

Statements by Iranians over the past few years , stating their intentions. The kind of service that the Americans, with all their hatred, have done us no superpower has ever done anything similar, Mohsen Rezai, secretary-general of the powerful Expediency Council that advises the Supreme Leader Ayatollah Khamanei, boasted on state television recently.

America destroyed all our enemies in the region. It destroyed the Taliban. It destroyed Saddam Hussein... The Americans got so stuck in the soil of Iraq and Afghanistan that if they manage to drag themselves back to Washington in one piece, they should thank God. America presents us with an opportunity rather than a threat — not because it intended to, but because it miscalculated. They made many mistakes.

Jerusalem - Iran reportedly told Palestinian Authority Prime Minister Ismail Haniyeh that Hamas should wait quietly for a dramatic Iranian announcement that is coming in a few months, the Hebrew daily Maariv reported. The Iranians also told Haniyeh to lower Hamas profile and calm the situation, the report said. Haniyeh met with Iranian President Mahmoud Ahmadinejad 11 days ago and received promises of economic aid and military cooperation as well as millions of dollars in cash. In four months, Iran is going to issue a statement that will dramatically change the strategic balance in the Middle East, the paper quoted Iranian officials as saying. The head of the Israels Mossad (secret service) Meir Dagan was quoted as telling Israeli lawmakers on Monday that

Ahmadinejad wants to have 3,000 centrifugal processors in bunkers by March 2007. The centrifuges enrich uranium, which can be used as fuel for a nuclear reactor but also is a key ingredient in the production of nuclear bombs. Experts here have warned that if Iran does acquire nuclear capability, it could then pursue its religious goal of spreading the Islamic revolution throughout the Middle East.

Commandant of Irans elite Islamic Revolutionary Guards Corps, Major General Yahya Rahim Safavi, said on state television. God willing, the 21st century will see the defeat of the U.S. and the Zionists, and the victory of freedom-seeking nations of the world. The final goal of the [1979] revolution is to create global Islamic rule and a regime of law to be led by the Imam Mahdi.

Here is what the advisor to thIm more worried about those crazy people running the show in Iran. The folks in charge of Iran think theyre going to cause their messiah to appear by them destroying US/Israel new Iranian president has said: The new Iranian President called for Israel to be annihilated. The first time a UN member actually called for the obliteration of another

The Iranian Presidents chief strategist, Hassan Abbassi, has come up with a war plan based on the premise that Britain is the mother of all evils – the evils being America, Australia, New Zealand, Israel, the Gulf states and even Canada, all of whom are the malign progeny of the British Empire. We have a strategy drawn up for the destruction of Anglo-Saxon civilization, says Mr Abbassi. There are 29 sensitive sites in the U.S. and in the West. We have already spied on these sites and we know how we are going to attack them... Once we have defeated the Anglo-Saxons the rest will run for cover.

The IRGC chief warned that Iran was seeing through critical days and fate-determining years. He described the purpose of Irans 1979 Islamic revolution as the Salvation of Muslims from the hands of the oppressive U.S. and Israel. commandant of Irans elite Islamic Revolutionary Guards Corps, Major General Yahya Rahim Safavi, said on state television, The final goal of the [1979] revolution is to create global Islamic rule and a regime of law to be led by the Imam Mahdi. God willing, the 21st century will see the defeat of the U.S. and the Zionists, and the victory of freedom-seeking nations of the world.

A Final Note:

Middle East leaders would like the United States to do something about Iran but are not sure what will happen if Iran is attacked. One of the Middle East leaders recently said by attacking Iraq the gates of hell have been opened and by attacking Iran it will push the Middle East into hell. On pondering Irans problem we must consider certain facts, this is a regime that is unfriendly to everyone starting with the Muslim Sunni Majority, one cannot reason with any nation or group whos beliefs are based on a militant ideology. The Shia belief of the Messiah the 12th Imam retuning after a World War like situation is very real. So is it possible Ahmedinejad is provoking a fight with the West, I believe this to be very accurate. We must remember he is a mouth piece for the Mullahs and could not have come to power without their blessing. This is a strongly held belief among the Radical Shia element that the Messiah is [Waiting] and will return after a World War like situation have broken out with the infidels. I am a Sunni Muslim and it trembles me.. I believe the West is truly justified in not allowing this regime to acquire Nuclear Weapons Capability. Iranian regime have been given plenty of chances to change their mind and alter their course. I predict this will lead the United States and the Allies into a Third World War , Iran has to choose between leading a cause or a nation, it is very capable of diffusing this escalation with the West, I dont believe Iran is willing to do that, I strongly feel that President George W. Bush should implement any contingency plans he may be given because it might be too late by the time the next President is inaugurated. Prudence dictates a policy of preemption in case diplomacy fails. a Nuclear Capable Iran is not an option.

August 16th 2007

Islamic Glossary used by the media

Arabic terms related to Islam has accompanied the upsurge of news about Middle Eastern and Southeast Asian terrorism in the last few years. Islamist radicals have hijacked the original intent of many Islamic terms, and Western media often misuse them. Here is a short list of those appearing frequently in the media, and in government speeches and documents.

Even though most of the worlds Muslims are not Arab, Islam originated in the Arabian peninsula among Arabic speakers. Arabic is the language of Islam in the same way that Greek is the language of Orthodox Christianity, and Hebrew the language of Judaism.

Term: Allah

Meaning: The proper name for God in Arabic, interchangeable with God as we use it in English. Christians and Muslim Arabic speakers use the word to refer to the monotheistic supreme being presumed to be God of the Muslims, Christians and Jews.

Term: Caliphate

Language: Englishization of Arabic *khalifa*

Meaning: An Islamic form of governance encompassing both administration of state affairs and leadership of the universal community of Muslims. The caliph, or successor (to Muhammad, Islams prophet and the first leader) heads this community. The last Islamic caliphate was the Ottoman Empire, which was abolished in 1924.

Term: Fatwa, or fetwa

Meaning: A formal legal opinion issued by a recognized religious legal authority.

Term: Islam

Meaning: submission or surrender.

Term: Jihad

Meaning: Struggle. Jihad refers, in many instances, to the internal struggle to live ones life in ethical accordance with Gods will. Its secondary meaning is external struggle—which might include war, but doesnt have to—to defend Islam against unbelievers. In its original usage, unbelievers only referred to other monotheists, Christians and Jews, and jihad was only contemplated in contexts where Islam was threatened.

Term: Hajj

Meaning: Annual pilgrimage to Mecca, which each Muslim must undertake at least once in a lifetime if he or she has the health and the wealth.

Term: <u>Hijab</u>

Meaning: Scarf worn on the head by Muslim women.

Term: <u>Imam</u>

Meaning: Leader in Arabic. The term is generally applied to religious leaders.

Term: <u>Mujahid/ Mujahideen</u>

Meaning: Struggler or striver on behalf of his faith. The term is associated most firmly with the Afghan guerrilla fighters who organized to oust the Soviet Army from Afghanistan in the 1980s.

Term: <u>Ramadan</u>

Meaning: The ninth month of the Lunar calender, month in which muslims are obligated to fast for thirty days Sunrise to Sunset.

Term: <u>Salafi/ Salafist</u>

Meaning: Someone who belongs to a reform movement with the goal of returning a corrupted Islam to its original ideals. Salafi movements have included a 19th century reform movement in Egypt, and the Saudi Salafi movement often called Wahhabism. Salafi movements have begun as efforts to reform Islamic practices they believe stray from Islams original intent. Some have become militantly anti-Western, but not all.

Term: Sharia

Meaning: Islamic canonical law, based on the Quran (Islams holy book) and other texts. Most observant Muslims living in Islamic societies find Sharia and secular laws compatible. Militant extremist groups and governments, such as the Taliban in 1990s Afghanistan, use Sharia law as a pretext for authoritarian rule.

Term: Shia [Shiite]

Meaning: Is a follower of the twelve Imams, Muslim sect that believes Ali and the Imams are the rightful successors of Muhammed and the concealment and Messianic return of the last recognized Imam.

Term: Sunni

Meaning: Muslim sect that adheres to the orthodox tradition and acknowledges the first four caliphs as rightful successors of Muhammed.

Term: Umma (ummah)

Meaning: The global Muslim community; the body of Muslim faithful.

Term: <u>Quran (Koran):</u>

Meaning: Recitation; according to Islam, the compiled verbatim words of Allah as dictated by Muhammad.

Index

al-Tariq al-Jawad,
Muhammad, 5
al-Zawahiri, Ayman, 99, 101
American Board of
Commissioners for Foreign
Missions, 135
Amir-Entezam, Abbas, 131
Amnesty International, 122
Anarak, 70
Anglo-Iranian Oil Company
(APOC), 137
Annan, Kofi, 54
Ansari, Ali M., 100
A.Q. Khan Nuclear Black Market,
164, 203–205
Arab League, 81
Arabs, 17, 23–24
Arafat, Yaser, 150
Arak, 70
Ardekan, 70
Aref, Mohammad Reza, 50
Armitage, Richard L., 163–164, 195
Asgarowladi, Habibollah, 128
Asgharzadeh, Ebrahim, 130
Ashura, 11, 86
Assembly of Experts, 36, 123–124
Assembly to Discern the Interests
of the State, 150
Association of Islamic Revolution
Loyalists, 128
Atomic Energy Organization of Iran
(AEOI), 208
Bonab, 70–71
Center for Agricultural Research
and Nuclear Medicine at
Hashtgerd, 74
Nuclear Technology Center of
Isfahan, 73
Tehran Nuclear Research Center
(TNRC), 75–76
Atomic Energy Research Center,
70–71
Atoms for Peace, 58
Atomstroyexport (ASE), 73, 211
Awaited One, 5

axis of evil, 100, 146
ayatollah, 4
Azarbaijan Democratic Party, 19
Azhari, 13
Azizi, Ebrahim, 116

Baath Party, 125
Bagdad, 4, 220
Bahonar, Mohammad Reza, 117
Bahonar, Muhammad Javad, 9
Bakhtiar, Shapour, 13–14, 131
Bakr, Abu, 1, 2
Baluchis, 21–22
Banisadr, Abolhassan, 113
Bank of Credit and Commerce
International, 168
Bank Sepah, 208
Baskerville, Howard, 136
Bazargan, Mehdi, 14
Baztab, 69
Bedlington, Stanley, 99
Beeman, William O., 68
Beg, Mirza Aslam
Abdul Qadeer Khan, 167, 185
Iranian nuclear weapons program,
190–192
Pakistan, 199
Benjamin, Samuel, 134
Berman, Ilan, 88
Besse, Georges, 61
Bhutto, Benazir, 165
Abdul Qadeer Khan, 162,
167–168, 185
North Korea, 171, 206
bin Laden, Osama, 95, 97–98
bin Laden, Saad, 95, 99, 101
Board of Civil Engineering
Faculty of the Science and
Technology University, 45, 46
Bolton, John, 66
Bonab, 70–71
Bonn firm, 59, 71
Boroujerdis, Ayatollah, 9
Boucher, Richard, 100, 192–193